ADDICTIVE RELATIONSHIPS
Reclaiming Your Boundaries

Joy Erlichman Miller

Health Communications, Inc.
Deerfield Beach, Florida

Joy Miller
Renewal
Peoria Heights, Illinois 61614

Library of Congress Cataloging-in-Publication Data

Miller, Joy Erlichman
    Addictive relationships.

    1. Interpersonal relations.   2. Self-actualization
(Psychology) I. Title.
HM132.M524   1989   158'.2   88-24419
ISBN 1-55874-003-1

ISBN 1-55874-003-1

Published by: Health Communications, Inc.
                3201 S.W. 15th Street
                Deerfield Beach, Florida 33442

Acknowledgments

REAL-ationships are a processs along my journey. My primary relationship with myself has been fostered and supported by you who have loved me unconditionally. As I became able to love myself, I became able to love you more.

Mom and Dad — The first knowledge of relationship occurs within our family of origin. I knew love was limitless and overflowing from my first breath. You have always given me a model to experience love, caring and appreciation. Sometimes, but not often enough, I tell you how much I love you and just how important you have been in my life. I give you my respect, my admiration and love for all that you have given me yesterday and today.

John — The door was open and you walked in. You taught me to trust, to feel, to love and believe. You are and always will be a cherished part of my journey "home." My path has been graced with your love. I will always love you and our bond is forever.

Heidi — No words can express what you have allowed me to unlock within myself. You taught me to accept my self *totally* and

iii

became my "living crystal" with a special love that I will treasure today and forever.

Joshua — Hold the feelings within you which make you so very special. Your love is like none other. Let no one take "you" from "you". Keep your gift and share your love, as you always have. I have given to you all I am — that is the greatest gift that I can give! My son, my son — my kingdom for my son . . . I love you, Boober!

Ade — Into my life the *real* you emerged. You have always given me the gift of insight and laughter. Your renewal of life has allowed me to watch YOU love yourself, as I always have.

Marie — You said to follow my heart. You inspired my dream and told me *I* was my only limitation. You have believed in me with a special care and love, and I affirm our connection in gratitude and thanks. My dear friend!

Laura — Into my life you entered once again — arms open, full of love. Nothing ever could destroy our bond. We found a place where we could be ourselves and love. Our dreams *are* our reality.

Friends and Clients — So many people have entered my life — each one of you has given me the gift of yourself. I cherish your gift and hold it tight within me. It is safe and I value your love and support.

Debbie — Some people stand and watch — but you have been there with support and caring and a gentle nudge to move me along my path. You gave me the room to be free and discover my heart. My gratitude and love.

Ruth — It is a "time for joy" because you entered my life — with light, love and hope.

Grandpa Bill, Bubby, Grandma Margie — From the past comes the future. You taught me intergenerational loving and you have never left my heart. In memory and in love.

Special Thanks — to all my dear friends at Health Communications and our family of authors, who have guided and enhanced my journey.

Contents

K. But I Believed In You (Trust Issues) 29

L. . . . Then They Will Respect Me
    (Self-Worth Determined By Others) 32

M. Please, Please Take Me With You
    (Fear Of Being Alone) 35

N. But You Should Do . . . (Societal Pressures) 38

O. Do You Think I Care If You Drink?
    (Home Of Origin Modeling) 40

P. What Will I Do Without You?
    (I'm Nothing Without A Relationship) 43

2. **Where Are We Going?** 47

    The Positives We Hold Within 47

    Finding The Balance 51

    Mirroring 56

    The Gift Of Self-Awareness 58

    Falling In Love With Yourself 61

3. **How Do We Get There?** 67

    You Get What You Got If You Do What You Did 68

    The 10 Demandments 73

    Relationship Boundaries 75

    Daily Progress Sheet 82

    Feelings Worksheet 88

    Breaking Distorted Shame Messages 94

    Chapter One — Your Story! 101

    Suggested Reading 107

Introduction

A Familiar Remembrance

Each week we eagerly awaited going to that unforgettable living room — it was almost like walking into our own home of origin. The familiar music moved us down the street and into the house that held us enmeshed with the family that became part of our being. The names of Edith, Archie, Gloria and the Meathead were like members of our own intimate family. We were as much a part of that family as any of the Bunkers. We became a sibling in the home that felt so comfortable and known.

At times we laughed, but more times than we may have cared to admit, we cried. In fact, many times we sobbed. We felt the pain and the dysfunction beneath the jokes and ridicule. Despite the haunting sarcasm of the laughter, we felt the deep sting of shame and pain each time we heard the words, "You Dingbat!" The feelings of the abuse hit just a tinge too close to our own pain. Scared and vulnerable, we quickly shut down emotionally, and tried to deny the similarities to our own personal histories.

Our family chameleon was Edith Bunker. She was the expert at sensing everyone else's needs, but lost to her own needs. Her entire world centered around others — her husband, her daughter, her son-in-law and her neighbors. Edith's caretaking and over-responsibility for everyone was the brunt of many farfetched jokes. But down deep if we really chose to let ourselves feel, we hurt for Edith. The pain engulfed our being because we knew the cruel reality — Edith had no awareness of her needs or desires. She had become totally camouflaged by her environment through devaluing her own existence.

Sometimes compulsive loving and its addiction can look humorous, in fact, even unbelievable to outsiders. Some believe it is a miraculous and gallant method of familial living. But, Edith knew the pain and despair of being out of synchronization with her own being. Many times, over and over, we shared her tears of despair because of her addictive loving style.

Toward the end of our life with the Bunkers, Edith did strive to claim her own personal boundaries. Boldly she struggled to fight the pressure and resistance of Archie with the encouragemment and support of Gloria and Michael. During those times of great fortitude, we applauded her strength when she believed in herself and the need to address her own issues. As the claiming of her personal boundaries expanded, a cruel twist of fate devastated our family image. Edith's premature death stole a dear family member away from our existence. We mourned and grieved what could have been, and what almost was. Edith gave all to love — but only briefly did she find the true love of herself.

This book is dedicated to the claiming of your personal boundaries and finding the strength within. We will journey forward and examine **where we are — where we are going** — and **how to get where we desire**. As our pathway moves onward, we will move from the limits of addictive relationships to the boundless potential of the greatest love of all — **the love of ourself**.

It is important to note as you travel along your journey, there are some important distinctions within this book. When we speak of addictive relationships, we are not looking at addictive relation-ships that center around just your spouse or your lover. You can have a destructive or addictive relationship with your children, your best friend or your parents. Destructive loving situations are not limited to just one aspect or person in your life. Be aware as you proceed that the relationships we are exploring are wide and expansive in nature. Do not limit your focus . . . if we have lost ourselves along the way, it is certain that we have most probably given ourselves away to a variety of different people.

Give yourself time, patience, love and understanding as you journey onward. Encourage yourself to look within without guilt and shame. You are following your destiny by trudging forward along your path. Our goal is to assist you on your way by creating the tomorrows of your dreams. We are on a quest together to find the limitless you. It has been said that you have no limits, only those which you have ascribed to yourself.

There may be some distracting jogs in the path along the way . . . but finding your strength and love within you is well worth the travel forward.

1

Where Are We?
Characteristics Of Destructive Relationships

A. "If I Tell Him I Love Him, He Will Change"
(Tunnel Vision)

Our destructive relationship is like traveling through a long airtight grey tunnel interspersed with a few brilliant specks of bright light. Despite the knowledge that we can leave the tunnel at any time, we continue searching aimlessly for another speck of iridescent light. Intellectually we know that the bright light might not be found for days, weeks or ever again — but the allure and challenge is too captivating. Despite the fact that the light brings joy for just a few moments, we find comfort in knowing that we can "feel" for those moments. Our fear is that the discontinuation of our journey might leave us empty and hollow, unable to feel anything except pain and agony. With each thought of discontinuing the search we feel a force within us that compulsively mandates us to continue our search forward.

The tunnel above illustrates a focus which totally encompasses another person. All of our thoughts seem to center around the significant person. Our mind races uncontrollably, dreaming of fantasies of our focused person. Despite our knowledge of the pain (broken promises, broken dreams) experienced in the relationship, we continue along the path. We find ourselves focusing on our dreams, or on the significant person's magnificent illusive words and not on the behaviors we have witnessed. We continue down the grey tunnel, searching for something outside ourselves to give us our inner serenity and the love we have always wanted.

"I settle for a crumb of what he has to offer. I hold on to that crumb like it is gold," described the sobbing Dodie. "If he has only five minutes in his busy day to give to me, I feel ecstasy of unbelievable proportions. The reality of the small pittance of time doesn't seem to matter. It is what he gives me. I can't live without it. I guess I don't think that I deserve any better, so I find myself settling for whatever I'm given. Men always have this effect on me — I have no control. Don't you understand? All I can think about is being with him for just one moment!"

Dodie's explanation of tunnel vision expresses the common threat experienced by destructive lovers. The mind appears powerless to attend to any other business except the fantasy of our lover. (This is not limited to lovers and can be experienced by any focus person who may be our spouse, friend or perhaps our own child.)

I give myself the gift of discovering a relationship of love with myself.

I am whole. I am complete. I am perfect just as I am right now.

B. "He Belongs To Me"
   (Propertyism)

Susan trembled as she spoke before the group. "Bill must share everything with me and no one else. I think that's what a perfect marriage is all about. Your husband tells you everything he does and feels. I *am* his wife you know!"

Engrossed with the need for control, Susan sees her husband, Bill, as her property. Marriage becomes suffocation. Independence, privacy and personal growth is deterred, in fact — feared. As long as Susan believes that Bill's disclosures will ensure the perfect marriage, she will continue to believe that this is the means to be "as one." United "as one" implies wholeness in Susan's mind.

This distorted thinking sets up a system of dependency and crippling effects. Our need to control and have a hold on another person is our means of protection from our fear of abandonment. The focus of our lives is outside ourselves, which consequently leaves us feeling scared, terrified and needy without our focus person. Consequently, if we hold someone tightly enough, we believe they won't leave us. Our fear unfortunately pushes that person into submission or further away.

Betsy, a member of an Adult Children of Alcoholics group, told of an incident in her childhood that reminded her of this truth. When she was six years old, Betsy spent what felt like years persuading her parents into getting her a bird. Although Betsy really wanted a dog or a cat, she came to love her bird even though she could not "play" with the bird. Betsy felt distant from the bird, talking to it through the limiting bars. She kept hearing her parents instructions echoing in her mind, "Don't let it out of the cage, it will fly away!" One day Betsy could no longer stand the bars that held the bird she loved. She reached inside and grabbed the bird, pulling it out of its cage. Immediately the bird attempted to fly and get free. Betsy, panicked at the thought of losing the bird, squeezed harder and harder as the bird attempted to fly away. Suddenly the bird stopped its struggle and went limp. Betsy's heart stopped beating as she became aware that in her attempt to restrain the bird, she had squeezed the life out of her beloved helpless pet.

Many times we do the similar squeezing in our relationships with people. The "object" of the "propertyism" (or should we say the "victim"?) feels the pain of strangulation. Being held too tightly, the victim eventually needs to escape because she feels like a captive — even if it's a captive of love. Ironically, we get just what we did not want. We find that our possessiveness sabotages our goal.

Sue Ellen told the group that being the victim of her husband's "propertyism" made her feel beaten down, useless, powerless and hopeless. She continued to explore the feelings which led to her passivity.

"I felt as if I couldn't breathe anymore. I tried to fight for air but I kept feeling as if I was continuously being held under water. I gasped for air, but I kept being pushed under over and over . . . again and again. I gave up trying to get away, it was just must easier. Now I don't know who I am — except a reflection of my husband. I don't think I have the power to find myself."

That which I hold on to, I lose. That which I release with love remains.

I am whole. I am complete. I am perfect just as I am right now.

C. "Tell Me Who I Am" (Externalization)

Filled with panic and fear Rachel believed she was nearing a nervous breakdown.

"I can't do anything without feeling the pain of not having him in my life. I must find a way to get him back." Rachel sobbed as she experienced the withdrawal symptoms of her addiction to her departed lover.

Compulsive destructive love is as addicting and devastating as alcohol and the withdrawal is as painful and as physically debilitating. Robin Norwood discusses in detail the similarities of alcoholism and compulsive loving in *Women Who Love Too Much* (Jeremy P. Tarcher, Inc., 1985). Both experience the common symptomology of physical ailments: sweating, physical pain, distorted thoughts and behavior, anger, delusions, lying, tunnel vision, obsession with the addictive substance and self-hatred.

Alcoholism and compulsive loving have a common element — a substance outside ourselves that we cannot control. Our focus is external in nature and, therefore, we will always be out of control. This is obvious because others can seldom fulfill our needs consistently.

Shakti Gawain's powerful book, *Living in the Light* (Whatever Publishing, Inc., 1986), relates the focus of externalism which ". . . results in disappointment, resentment and frustration. Either these feelings build up constantly and cause emotional strife or they are suppressed and lead to emotional numbness."

As long as we depend totally on something outside ourselves, we will continue the pattern of self-destruction and emotional withdrawal and pain.

---------------■---------------

I must build a loving relationship with myself before I can share my gift with others.

I am whole. I am complete. I am perfect just as I am right now.

---------------■---------------

D. "Fiddle-Dee-Dee"
(Hope/Fantasy/Distortion)

Seeing reality as it really is can be an extremely painful and devastating event. Ignoring the reality and saying "Fiddle-dee-dee" to the situation allows us to evade the real situation and its true pain (which requires us to make a change to take care of *our* needs). Many of us cover our pain and in fact prolong its hold. By refusing to feel and view the reality as it truly is, our emotional despair grows in intensity and becomes overwhelming.

A perfect example of this concept is the pain of separation and divorce experienced by an Adult Child of an Alcoholic (ACoA) named Christy. Faced with her decision to leave her drug-abusing, physically abusive husband, Christy threw herself into a relationship with another married man. She immersed herself in the hope of his leaving his unfulfilling wife which promoted her distortion and fantasy. By getting out of her heart (pain) and escaping into her head (fantasy), Christy prolonged and intensified her stress and trauma. Totally immersed in her new ideal relationship, she denied her feelings and the real issues which prohibited her ability to look at what she was doing. She was living with blinders on — seeing only what she wanted to see, believing her dream would unfold. Christy cautiously admitted that she was . . . "walking down a narrow path, oblivious to the surroundings which were filled with users, deceptions, lies and manipulations."

Overwhelmed with her distortion and inner chaos, Christy was confronted by her relationship group. Breaking through her denial, she eventually discovered and accepted the fact that she was terrified to be responsible for herself. Christy realized that she had never been totally responsible for herself in her life. Men had always been there to depend upon to fill her every need.

This pattern of dependency led to lowered self-esteem and decreased self-worth. Consequently, her dreams of another man rescuing her was easier than facing the reality of being totally in control of her own life.

The gift I give myself is the belief that I can follow my journey and trust my inner self.

I am whole. I am complete. I am perfect just as I am right now.

E. "I'm Sure This Will Work"
(Power Plays/Manipulation)

"I wrote the book on manipulation and game-playing," said Mandy. "I learned that sickness gains attention as do tears, helplessness, sad looks and acting naive. If I act like a sweet-talking innocent child, I most generally get my way," she proclaimed proudly. Mandy described a complex combination of power plays which included silence, sexual promiscuity, withdrawal of sex, blaming, taking on blame, passivity and nagging. Each has its benefits she explained in therapy. She continued to explore the "tricks" she learned from her mother and sisters who utilize them with great mastery.

Without the power plays, game-playing and manipulation, many of us feel naked and unarmed in a relationship. It appears that the guiding force to fulfilling our needs is gone without these devices. Without the trusted behaviors and actions, we have no model from which to draw upon, as well as no insight into acquiring our needs. Our family of origin taught us about destructive relationships, not healthy ones. The process of learning the needed skills to finding true wholeness and happiness is exchanged for the development of manipulative skills which create destructive loving.

Commonly, as children of trauma, we learn to utilize people-pleasing, martyrdom and rationalizations in our repertoire of skills. Earnie Larson in *Stage II Recovery, Life Beyond Addictions* (Winston Press, 1985) effectively discusses how these characteristic types are self-destructive. Each of the types has a common bond — the focus is on another person, not ourselves. Consequently, we do not take into account our needs, values, wants or strengths and, therefore, give up ourselves in the quest for another's approval and loving.

---■---

I can be honest and direct in communicating my needs to others.

I am whole. I am complete. I am perfect just as I am right now.

---■---

F. "But It Worked In The Past!"
(Regression To Old Behaviors)

"I know she's not the woman for me . . . I mean she has hurt me so much! I loved her though!" A handsome, but physically worn ACoA named Dave discussed his feelings about his separated spouse.

"She's done all of this before — the deceit, the lies, the manipulation . . . but the good times are so wonderful — so full of magical electricity." Dave, like many of us, slip back into old familiar destructive loving, neglecting our own boundaries as we attempt to keep our love connection. Despite our knowledge of the past, we get caught in words that are offered up, not behaviors that we witness. Our heart allows us to follow the distortion of the words that destroy us.

Carol mourned the loss of her unfaithful lover and found herself regressing to teenlike actions. She reported to her group that she drove by Bill's home repeatedly (to check if he had a date), continuously called his house' and hung up, and lay awake night after night thinking only of the past. Carol confessed that she had mentally written hundreds of scripts to get Bill back, but to no avail. Beaten down, Carol returned to therapy to develop a trust and love for herself.

Our destructive patterns are difficult to break. They appear to be all we know and have seen modeled. These destructive tendencies are the only way we have been able to attain our needs. The media has taught us that the manipulative behavior we see on television (ie, *Dallas, Knots Landing,* Daytime Soaps, *Falcon Crest*) always works for the acquisition and retention of our conquest — the perfect love. Consequently, the television media has built a distorted illusion which may boost their ratings, but destroys our ability to be real and intimate with ourselves and others. We become confused about the elements of a normal relationship and learn to continue the destruction we saw modeled in our homes of origin. Our fears of abandonment, due to our unmet childhood needs, keep us locked into obsessive compulsive loving. Unfortunately, our relationships become addictive and destructive, rather than healthy and nurturing.

Today I will respect and love myself by recognizing my own needs first.

I am whole. I am complete. I am perfect just as I am right now.

G. ". . . And You Will Marry Me!" (Mind-Reading)

"I know that he wants only me." This is the mental attitude of the destructive loving mind reader. To fulfill this dream, many of us have found ourselves plotting how we can give the loved one just what he needs. We believe that by giving our focus person what he truly desires, he will want only us.

Becky spoke of her clandestine schemes of reading and scripting just what Bill desired.

"I know that if I give myself to him in a certain way, he'll be all mine." Becky believed she could magically mind read what Bill wanted, needed and desired without the elements of a healthy relationship — time, patience, communication and nurturing. Her dysfunctional home of origin had taught her the importance of mind-reading, as well as the need for external focusing. Becky avoided reading her own mind (and heart) and focused on reading others.

Mind-reading sets up a process of distorted messages, broken dreams, fantasy and disappointment. Our early training taught us always to be aware of everyone's eyes. We become watchful of other people's smallest moves which would indicate their mood. Like chameleons, we allowed this hypervigilance to determine which way we should behave. (It should be noted that we can expand the frame of reference from not just hypervigilancy but to that of hypersensitivity. Many of us have become hyperaudio, hypersensitive to touch and hyper to a variety of other stimuli.)

Our hypervigilance gave us an early warning system to prepare us for impending danger and our need to change our behavior at a moment's notice. We started to rely on that high-powered watchfulness to protect us from pain and shame. Because of our hyperalertness, which was learned in our dysfunctional home of origin, we believe that it is necessary to read everyone who enters our life. Consequently, we were trained in our home of origin to enter relationships without communication — we learn to react, not act.

Earnie Larson in *Stage II Recovery* (Winston Press, 1985) describes a distorted causal triangle, which illustrates how many of us behave in a destructive pattern. Typically when *an event* occurs, we *react* first and then *think* after we see the consequences of our action. The causal diagram looks like the following:

EVENT >>>REACT >>> THINK

The above process is destructive because we react before we think. That is, we do not internalize or check our response before we respond. This black and white decision-making process encourages our mind-reading, despite its devastating results (Figure 1). We learn to be *reactors* to each situation based on our past old destructive patterns. We become externalizers not internalizers. We are out of touch with our own needs and act out of inner shame, pain and fear.

Figure 1. Destructive Reaction

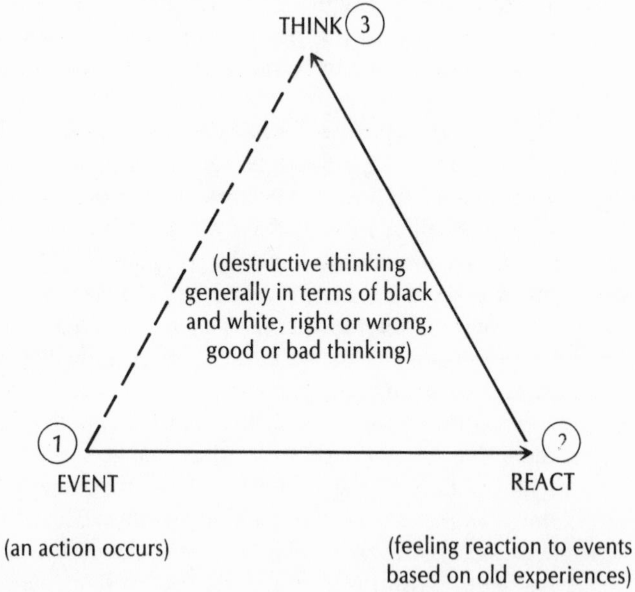

THINK (3)

(destructive thinking
generally in terms of black
and white, right or wrong,
good or bad thinking)

(1)   (?)
EVENT   REACT

(an action occurs)   (feeling reaction to events
                                         based on old experiences)

In comparison Figure 2 illustrates a process that is healthy. When something occurs, we think, evaluate and feel, then weigh our decisions — then we respond. *We internalize before we externalize.* The diagram in this case would be as follows.

EVENT >>> THINK >>> RESPOND

We *read* our own minds and our heart, and then we make a decision that takes in account our feelings. We use our values to clarify what we want in each situation. The triangle in Figure 1 would differ for a healthy relationship and would be viewed in the following manner (see Figure 2).

Figure 2. Healthy Reaction

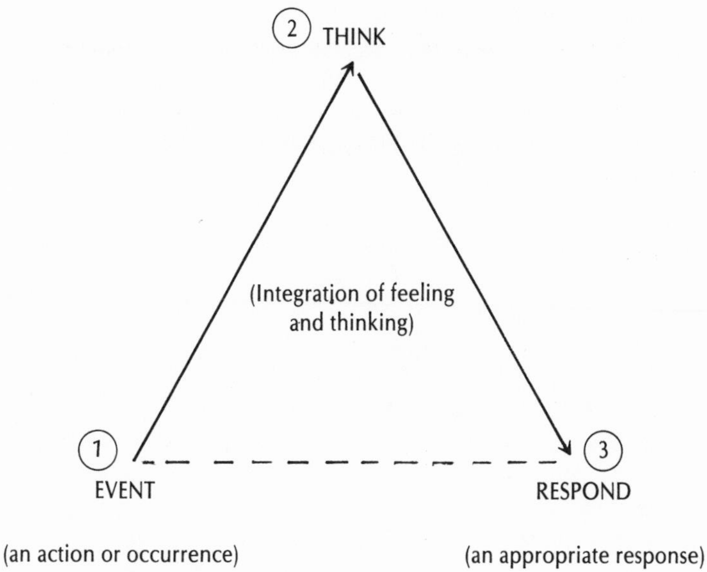

As we saw in Figure 1, our attraction to dysfunctional people creates a pattern of mind-reading which assists our destructive loving. We believe that we automatically know what other people are thinking, as well as what they desire. We move in quickly and begin to be over-responsible for their behavior and well-being. Our caretaking encourages us to take our focus off ourself and place it on the other person. We find that it is necessary to be "in control" of the relationship because of our need to "be in control." The mind-reading is necessary to stay on top of the situation, just as it was in our childhood.

Confused by the abandonment of her live-in lover, Paula broke down in session. "I've done everything for that man. How could he possibly leave me? I've given him everything . . . even before he asked for it."

Paula's loss of her lover created an imminent nervous breakdown. What Paula had not learned is fundamental for healthy communication — checking out the reality of what you think or feel. If Paula had integrated this skill of "reflection", she would have known that she was not effectively communicating. (Reflection is a process of breaking down aspects of communication and checking with the other person to find out if your impressions are correct and on target.)

Communication, like any other life skill, needs to be learned. The components of healthy communication involve the elements of listening, reflecting, restating, decision-making and values clarification. Without this vital training we are walking a tightrope without a safety net.

The gift I give to myself is reading my own mind and attending to my needs first.

I am whole. I am complete. I am perfect just as I am right now.

H. "I'll Take You Away From It All!" (Caretaking)

"I've tried and tried to please my daughter-in-law. I find myself bending over backwards to do anything just to get her to like me, but it's useless." Patty confidently declared, "If only my daughter-in-law would realize her Adult Children issues and break through her denial, I *know* she would be so much happier." Patty, nearing her breaking point, was exasperated as she continued telling of her pain. "I have so much I could share and give to her. My recovery program would surely bring our family together." (Once again note that a destructive relationship can occur between lovers, a spouse, your children, a friend, your family, etc.)

Patty's painful experiences were discussed in group as the other members confronted her caretaking behavior. Patty, who was an Adult Child married to a recovering alcoholic, had not realized the extensiveness of her pattern of caretaking. She was very familiar with the responsible caretaking role which she had perfected before her recovery. Surprised at the recurring destructive behavior, Patty discovered that she was now trying to please and take care of her ACoA daughter-in-law.

Our homes of origin were enmeshed and cemented in dysfunction with caretaking behaviors. Those of us who are females were also inducted into the societal expectations of caring for males in our life. As firstborn female children, the pressures and responsibilities to care for others led many of us into a double bind of destructive loving.

The media, through television, movies and books, has taught us that romance is enhanced by those who care for others. Some of our early training revolved around such models as *Donna Reed* (always caring for her family's every need with an apron, dress and heels on), *I Love Lucy* (she was always manipulating the world to take care of her husband's career), *I Dream of Jeannie* (a woman whose only role was to wait on and please her lover in a seductive manner), Beach Party movies (taught us about women who devotedly care and wait on the shore for their adventuresome males). Disney movies illustrated women like *Cinderella* and *Snow White* who cleaned and cared for others and were rewarded with personal beauty and handsome princes who rode to their rescue. But alas, the rewards of caretaking behaviors are only fantasies. As we have discovered, caretaking leads to focusing on the needs of others at the expense of diminishing or ignoring our own needs.

People-pleasing leads to personal resentment, stuffed feelings, despair, inner turmoil and self-hatred. Our actions are oftentimes dictated strictly by our feelings, not by our rational thinking. We become prisoners of our own created misery.

———————————■———————————

The gift I give to myself is taking care of myself and believing in my own worth.

I am whole. I am complete. I am perfect just as I am right now.

———————————■———————————

I. "A Fatal Attraction"
(Going Against Values/Morals)

To gain John's attention, Cindy was willing to do anything, including marry another man she did not love. Her hope and fantasy was that John would run to her side and beg her to marry him instead. Passion would surely bring John to his senses, and he would be compelled to rescue Cindy from impending romantic disaster. Unfortunately, John never did rescue Cindy from any crisis. Going against her own values and acknowledging her self-destructive values did not change John's actions or thoughts.

Similarly, the destructive pattern of our unhealthy attraction toward people in our lives rarely achieves what we really desire. Instead, we find ourselves filled with anger and resentment toward others, and ultimately ourselves. That internal anger adds fuel to our pattern of self-defeating behavior. If we can't be true to ourselves, how can we possibly be true to a relationship?

Sara, a compulsive lover, went against her religious beliefs by becoming emotionally involved with a married man. Despite her strong religious convictions, her own unfulfilling marriage was but a continuation of her unmet needs from every man in her life. The strength of her Higher Power now became her enemy in the face of what she desired — an unavailable married man. The cycle was intensified by the minimal satisfaction that this married man could guarantee. Despite this realization, the passion within her still existed. With him in her life she could *feel!* Feeling alive was what she lacked in her marriage to her husband. In her unfulfilling marriage, she only experienced negative feelings of failure, disappointment, pain and despair in herself. In comparison, with her lover she lived in her inner child who wanted a man to love and care for her. The correlation to her unfulfilled needs with her alcoholic father only confused her heart and caused her to shut the door on reality. Unwilling to face her own issues and pain, Sara fell in love with a man who could never be hers.

As a result of this conflict with her morals and religious beliefs, she manifested physical and emotional losses. Physically she began self-destructive behavior by bodily harming herself as she drew nearer and nearer to helplessness, hopelessness and a suicidal ideology. Emotionally the conflict created immense depression, grief and pain. Sara almost took her own life because she could not have the man in her fantasy and illusion.

Amazingly, many of us discover that we will give up parts of our being as easily as cutting off a body limb to gain or maintain a relationship. In fact, we *do* cut off parts of ourselves as we focus on others. We give away our heart, our soul, our desires and our needs to others. Ultimately we lose our belief in ourself in the hope that we can attain our elusive lover. As we do this, we become what others desire. In the process we become less whole in the hope of gaining a whole, complete relationship. To our despair, we realize our destructive tendencies *after* we have given up all that we are, only to gain another incomplete needy partner.

The gift I give to myself is valuing and allowing myself to be my primary relationship.

I am whole. I am complete. I am perfect just as I am right now.

J. "I Will Win You Over."
(Chase For A Prize)

Kenneth sat forward in his chair amazed by his revelation. "I only want to be in a relationship when there is something to win. I *need* to attain the prize. It's all a game — don't you see? I need to master the relationship and gain control. When I win the conquest and capture her love, she becomes dependent and needy and then I lose interest. The chase is over and I'm triumphant once again. There is no more excitement, no more thrill for me. I find myself wanting to move on to someone else who looks like a challenge and a means of excitement."

The cycle was repeated over and over for Kenneth despite his lack of intimacy in each relationship. The cycle of destruction created inner pain and agony for Kenneth, who believed he was deficient as a man. He concluded that he was not capable of true love. The reality of the situation was that Kenneth *could not love anyone else* because of his lack of love for himself. The challenge of the chase was actually the challenge of finding what he needed inside himself. As long as Kenneth searched for others to fill his emptiness inside, he would continue his destructive patterns of self-hatred, despair and failure. These feelings haunted his emotional stability.

Kenneth recalled as a child how his father would bring home one candy bar for his brother and him to share. Initially he remembered how he would allow his brother to break the candy bar in half and choose a piece. It didn't matter the size of the broken piece because whichever one his brother chose was the one he wanted. Kenneth had learned and reinforced the message that he wanted what the other person had at the time. The game of relationships became one of outsmarting the other person to fill your own needs. Kenneth learned that the conquest came in how well you could play the game to attain the prize you desired.

Kenneth's response to conquered relationships is quite common for many of us. We seem to be "hooked" into the passion, excitement, thrill and intensity of gaining someone else's trust and elusive love. This is the ultimate revival of our home of origin. Once again we challenge ourselves to gain control of love — the love we could not attain from our parents. We search out love through others to somehow fill the void created by the missing love of our early childhood years. We relentlessly search onward in an eternal journey, unconsciously trying to attain our needs through others. Unfortunately, we do not see the difference between a true intimate growing relationship and the challenge of breaking through the vulnerabilities of other people.

The prize that I give to myself is the gift of loving myself.

I am whole. I am complete. I am perfect just as I am right now.

K. "But I Believed In You!"
(Trust Issues)

Many of us find that we are at complete dichotomies in our relationships — *trusting too much or not trusting at all.* In most cases we continue along a path of trust until we collide with a trauma and typically go to the opposite extreme. From black to white and back again we see no other options for our relationships. Repeatedly we trust one person in a relationship past our boundaries to discover that in the next relationship we go to the other end of the spectrum and do not trust at all. We live in the extremes and maintain no relationship which has healthy boundaries or middle ground within the spectrum. Our extremes lock us into our own personal destruction.

A recently divorced woman named Dawn told of her destructive relationship in which she trusted to extremes. In fact, she trusted her unfaithful husband so much that she was oblivious to an affair right before her eyes. Despite phone calls from the "other woman" to her house, she believed that she could depend on her husband to be loyal and true to only her. Denial and trust in his hope of changing kept her locked into a path of self-destruction. The fear of looking squarely at the truth kept Dawn locked into low self-esteem and helplessness.

After this experience of trauma and pain, Dawn swore she would never love or trust another person. Tightly she locked the door to her heart. No one was allowed inside the door which held the woman who desperately wanted love. This opposite reaction is as destructive as its counterpart action of trusting too much.

Many men and women relate to Dawn's denial and inappropriate trust. It appears that we get involved too deeply or too quickly in the hope of attaining what we truly need — love. Our enthusiasm to gain externally what we do not hold internally (love of self) drives us toward an elusive relationship. Despite mixed messages and the signs of reality, we strive to make each relationship "perfect". Our fear of being alone, and our need for acceptance catches us in our own sticky entangling web of trusting beyond our boundaries. The body fights to keep us aware, but our fears which feel so scary, keep us blinded.

We fear that if we don't hang on and trust the relationship we have, no matter how destructive, there will be nobody else for us. But the old lesson rings true — *if we do what we did, we get what we got.* In effect we turn over our boundaries to other people, who hold them in their powerful hands. *They* become the master of *our* destiny. We become victims of our own creation. Consequently we tend to create in our minds our perfect savior, relentlessly setting ourselves up for more pain and anguish.

When we look back at our homes of origin, we realize we had poor models of healthy relationships. Without a map to show us the way, we journey blindly down our parents' path. The destruction we witnessed in our childhood becomes our own destiny. Locked in our inner dream, we trust those who do not deserve our trust. We live for a small handout to rekindle our unrealistic illusions and fantasies. Searching endlessly we plod onward to find someone who can comfort and nurture our child within.

As I learn to trust myself, I can learn to trust appropriately.

I am whole. I am complete. I am perfect just as I am right now.

L. ". . . Then They Will Respect Me"
(Self-Worth Determined By Others)

As we journey through life, we search for someone to provide our missing puzzle piece in hope of completing the elusive picture of total happiness. Many of us desperately continue our destructive pattern of looking outside ourselves for worth, esteem and value. Our journey has taken us into places we dared NOT return to over and over again. We have discovered that we have a pattern of continuously choosing mates who are replays of our dysfunctional home of origin. To our dismay, we discover that we have unconsciously chosen people who recreate our challenge to attain the love of our unloving parent from our home of origin. Over and over again we attempt as adults to gain the elusive love that we could not attain in our childhood. This time we attempt to "do it right". This time we attempt to give all we have to the relationships and disregard our boundaries — surely this will allow others to love us as we desire.

Anita, a shy timid woman, spoke of her attempt to find a meaningful love. "I keep trying to fill the void within me — I feel so empty inside. I thought the love of a man would make me feel whole."

Anita gave up her home, her family and most painfully, herself, to marry a man who took her from her homeland of Mexico. After months of therapy Anita broke through her pain and discovered that the void within was the love of herself. Without truly loving who she was, Anita could only feel incomplete and partial. Anita found that she held what she needed within herself. She discovered that she must face the pain of her separation and trust in herself. Peace and serenity came after Anita found the strength, power and her own value within.

The phenomenon of external referencing is a common characteristic of children of trauma. In our first book, *Following the Yellow Brick Road: An Adult Child's Personal Journey Through Oz* (Health Communications, 1988), we help the readers discover their own positive attributes. You soon will find that you, too, hold such miracles within yourself. The key to finding these miracles is to recognize the one simple truth: Your worth is determined totally by you. *You have all you need within.*

Sometimes we wear blinders when it comes to our own inner abilities as well as our needs. Louise Hay, in her best seller, *You*

Can Heal Your Life (Hay House, 1987), states, "Love is the miracle cure and loving ourselves works miracles in our own life."

Consequently, the greatest gift that we can attain stays locked deep within us. The treasures that we have hidden deep within become covered with cobwebs and dust created by years of neglect. Our recovery is surely halted when we look outside ourselves for self-esteem and value.

———————————■———————————

I am enough. I will find what I need inside myself.

I am whole. I am complete. I am perfect just as I am right now.

———————————■———————————

M. "Please, Please Take Me With You!" (Fear Of Being Alone)

For many of us the devastating thought of abandonment is part of our every waking moment. In fact, many of our dreams and fantasies encompass finding someone who will never leave us. Our fear of abandonment mandates our deceit, manipulation and self-destructive behaviors to extinguish the pain of feeling alone. As ACoAs or Children of Trauma, we will hold on to any relationship, even if it is one that is fabricated in our minds. We tend to hide reality from ourselves in order to maintain the dream that someone loves us. The shocking fact that the focus of our attentions does not love us in the way we want is too painful to believe or accept.

Betty, an attractive woman who has been plagued by many destructive relationships, kept men around her so she would not feel.

"As long as I am with a man, I don't have to look at 'me.' " Betty described the pain that emerged when she was alone as similar to withdrawal from drugs. She continued to explain that the fear of being alone made her feel insecure and incomplete.

Betty tearfully related, "I feel like there is a big hole in me and the wind is rushing through me — I feel hollow and hungry without a man." She related that the hole was so large when she was alone, that she quickly ran to attain a dose of love from any man who was willing to give her a small pittance of attention.

It appears that the fear of abandonment is so intensely destructive that we will do almost anything to feed our emotional starvation. This starvation was such a powerful experience in our homes of origin that we were always giving in an attempt to gain attention, a look, a praise or a hug. Inconsistently, the giving and people-pleasing allowed us to attain some satisfaction in getting our needs met. Unfortunately, the inconsistency taught us a destructive pattern of giving and giving and *giving* and *GIVING* past the point of sanity, to feed our emotional starvation. But our deepest fear that no one ever knew was our fear of not meeting expectations and having someone walk away. We knew they would abandon us because we were not enough. This conviction of "not being enough" appears to be the most destructive message which is tied into fears of abandonment.

We learned in early childhood that love is gained from outside ourselves. Love was an external commodity that had to be earned or won. A co-dependent home does not teach us the skills of loving ourselves — quite the contrary. Co-dependent homes teach us the destructive concept that we are nothing without our focus person. In fact, in an odd fashion, we become numb to our own needs. We never ask for what we desire. Instead we give in an attempt to gain.

A responsible Adult Child named Anne learned she was meaningful and loved only for what she accomplished. Her accomplishments fed her emotional starvation, but only with crumbs of nourishment. Destructive as it might be, at least the crumbs she attained in a relationship were some type of nourishment. Unfortunately, it didn't seem to matter that Anne was not meeting her own needs. She pointed out in session that the problem was not learning to ask for her needs, but even *acknowledging* that she had needs at all.

For some of us, the fear of abandonment has ambivalent or mixed feelings associated within. As victims of physical, verbal or sexual abuse, we have intensely divergent feelings of fearing and hoping for abandonment all in the same breath. On one hand, abandonment meant safety, discontinuation of pain and protection from the abuse. On the other hand, abandonment meant we would truly be physically alone with all of our feelings. Overwhelmed with these conflicting feelings, we tend to create and attract relationships that have no boundaries, no endings and no consistency about what is acceptable and appropriate within a relationship.

I have found the child within and I am not alone. My gift is deep within me.

I am whole. I am perfect. I am complete just as I am right now.

N. "But You Should Do . . ." (Societal Pressures)

Society puts many pressures on us concerning relationships, but possibly the most intense pressure is the need to be involved in a relationship. Many of us desperately feel required to be "spoken for" to fit into our pre-established societal role. We also feel the pressures of our physiological age, our biological ticking clock, our parental attitudes (our should-ers) or our role placement within our family of origin. We allow external pressures to intensify our internal pressure. We believe that we must have someone love us to fill our unmet needs that we choose not to fill ourself. Society's intensity gets greater and greater, while our pain and fear of being totally alone encourages our leap into destructive relationships.

An Adult Child named Rita was nearing hysteria as she sobbed, "At least I have someone! He might not be the best man in the world for me, but at least I have someone who cares, at least *part* of the time. I know that he doesn't meet my expectations or fill my emotional needs, but I'm so scared to be alone and feel!"

Rita discovered that her lover reminded her of her alcoholic father. Every man in her life had been unable to give her what she needed because *she* could not give herself what she needed.

Society has instilled the belief that we are less than whole if we are not involved with someone. We are scrutinized as having a defect, or perhaps our sexual orientation is questioned, or we are made to feel like we are incapable of maintaining a relationship. This self-destructive message system once again creates more pressure inside. As the fire within us heats up, our self-hatred and fear blazes out of control. The flames rage, and quickly we feel like we will be incinerated by our own mind and society's crushing hand, our heart and feelings locked tightly with a large padlock to hold back the pain and despair. Unfortunately, we believe that the only way to unlock the chain that binds us is to become involved with another person. This neediness encourages our belief to become involved in a relationship without first having a healthy relationship with ourself.

I am the master of my destiny. I will listen and follow only my heart-felt shoulds.

I am whole. I am complete. I am perfect just as I am right now.

---

0. "Do You Think I Care If You Drink?"
   (Home Of Origin Modeling)

The correlation between children of alcoholics/dysfunctional families and compulsive relationships have been verified by many authors including Janet Woititz, Robin Norwood and Susan Forward. Our alcoholic/dysfunctional home was filled with inconsistencies, unmet needs, defective parental modeling, lack of skill development, grief and loss. This has encouraged us to follow our compulsive loving patterns within our lives.

Because we did not get our needs met as children, we search throughout the remainder of our life trying to get our needs filled by someone outside ourself. It appears to be the ultimate challenge that feels so comfortable. We realize painfully that our dysfunctional parents were not physically or emotionally available for us in our home of origin. Because of the missing love in our childhood, we search out someone to fill the empty hollow hole within us. Unfortunately, we are typically attracted to people who are not only dysfunctional, but needy, and most often other nonrecovered Children of Trauma. The attraction has such magnitude, that the forces between us feel right. Because our home of origin has taught us to ignore the reality of situations, we learned to become extremely tolerant of inappropriate behaviors. We listen to our focus person's words and do not look at the inconsistent behavior that we see in the other person. We find ourself not claiming our own boundaries because of our fears (abandonment, failure, not being good enough, not doing it right, etc.). Our neediness encourages our caretaking and over-responsibility. Filled with shame and loss, we reach out for anyone who appears to have an interest in us as a person. The most revealing manifestation of our addictive loving style is our attraction to someone who is alcoholic, abusing or dysfunctional.

Lorna found herself once again attracted to another active alcoholic. "I hadn't realized how they all had fit the same pattern. No wonder the relationships all had a familiar ring — they all are so similar to my alcoholic father — they even physically resemble him."

It seemed that as quickly as Lorna broke off a relationship with one man, she just as quickly found another dysfunctional man to take his place. The dust had not settled from the first man before the replacement moved into Lorna's life. By moving men in quickly, Lorna did not have to evaluate her destructive pattern of loving or the pain of her feelings. Lorna denied what was so obvious — her home of origin's alcoholism still had a powerful and gripping effect on her relationships today.

———————————■———————————

I give myself the gift of living in the moment and loving my existence.

I am whole. I am complete. I am perfect just as I am right now.

———————————■———————————

P. "What Will I Do Without You?" (I'm Nothing Without A Relationship)

Vera planned her separation from her husband for months. Carefully she explored all the reasons for her decision to ask Ted to leave. His relapse with alcoholism was just one reason for her conclusion. Her four children needed consistency in their lives, as did Vera. As Ted neared the date of his leaving, Vera became increasingly more involved in his departure planning. Unconsciously Vera started to enable Ted's sabotaging of the departure. The children who had supported and encouraged the separation, quickly changed directions and pleaded for reconciliation. Despite Vera's planning and commitment, she became fearful that she would be nothing without a relationship. Her fears of facing the world without a man in her life created terror and an uncontrollable need to keep Ted close. She was so terrified by the thought of being alone that she was willing to live in the dysfunction to keep things the same. Confronted by relationship group members, Vera's anxiety, sabotaging and procrastination were addressed. She realized that she did have the power to be responsible and safe with the person she had in her life. She was not alone or without a relationship because she had *herself.*

Without a partner in our life, many of us feel incomplete and empty. The fear of truly being alone and facing life's responsibilities becomes a terror. To extinguish our fear of failure and pain we find ourself holding on to a destructive relationship. Unfortunately the pain is most always not worth the gain. Most Adult Children admit that they know the pain and disappointment they will experience in the relationship — it is comfortable. It's like walking through familiar garbage in a dumpster — we choose to stay in the dumpster, even if it is filled with smelly garbage. Our fear is that if we jump out of the dumpster, we will have no frame of reference and will fail in the outside world.

Inevitably the unknown situation of being without a relationship is uncomfortable and scary — so we stay in the garbage can. We can make no change in our life until we are willing to make changes. The quote rings once again in our ears — "If you do what you did, you get what you got!"

Personal transformation does occur when we allow our awareness to expand. *You* have made a change in this moment by allowing *your* awareness to be open to all that you have found

within this chapter. You can open the door to change and risk
stepping beyond one's comfortable boundaries of doing what you
have always done before. This exploration of your personal needs
and wants does seem scary. We totally understand, but you *will* find
what you need. Just look inside and trust.

I am not alone as long as I have a relationship with myself. My gift is learning about the power of love within.

I am whole. I am complete. I am perfect just as I am right now.

2

$$\diamond$$

Where Are We Going?

The Positives We Hold Within

Reflect back for a moment . . . take yourself back to your teens . . . perhaps you were like us — one of the lovesick teens of the '60s? The Crystals, The Supremes and Lesley Gore filled our hearts with the messages of love and romance. We were told over and over that we must do *anything* to keep our man. There was "no mountain too high", and "we were yours until the stars fell from the sky." We believed Little Peggy March when she told us to "follow him wherever he might go" despite our feelings or our needs because "he *was* our destiny."

Over and over our generation was reminded that we must give *all* to love. Love became the entity that we had to have at any cost — the ultimate fatal attraction. Unfortunately as we pursued our love, we lost our connection to what we held inside. In fact, we numbed ourselves to the point that we lost sight of all of our positive qualities. We were in pursuit of an elusive romance at the cost of our own being.

We possessed many admirable and desirable characteristics needed for a meaningful relationship, but we took those positive characteristics to extremes. We allowed our positives to become negatives because of their intensity. Our positives became destructive and crippling. Our love became a dependency . . . our devotion became compulsive . . . and our life became unmanageable and out of control. The control of our lives was taken over by a nonexistent dream which entrapped and framed our experience.

Our positive characteristics are numerous, but they must be balanced in each of us. An example of balancing is caring for another person. The extreme of the positive characteristic of caring is caretaking. Caring for another is balanced, but caretaking (taking control and feeling responsible for that person) is a destructive extreme within the spectrum.

Examples Of The Spectrum

Apathy	Caring	Caretaking
Irresponsible	Responsible	Over-responsible
Justify	Encourage	Nag
Rejection	Accept	Control
Withhold	Communicate	Dominate
Alienate	Understand	Possessive
Naive	Honest	Manipulative
Boundless	Flexible	Rigid

Without the balancing within the spectrum our lives become self-destructive and we travel on a compulsive path, destroying our relationships with our own self. If we are not balanced within, we become unbalanced with all of our relationships in general.

Our balancing and centering takes constant vigilance, risk-taking, listening to our inner voice, experimentation and patience. We must allow ourself the privilege of standing "like an observer" on the outside to watch our own behavior. This process mandates that we discover how we act, and record our feelings and reactions to the behaviors we witness.

An analogy might be like standing along a train track watching a passing freight train as each boxcar passes with its contents open for inspection. As we observe the contents, we evaluate our personal feelings and thoughts about what we visualize in the passing cars. With these insights we learn to track and record our feelings and defocus from the passing train. The focus becomes an internal mirror of what we feel inside. We become the "engineer" of our own life and view things on a larger more holistic viewpoint.

This concept can be utilized by taking small steps in a relationship and checking out our reactions to our risk-taking. It involves constantly checking our feelings and allowing them to surface for examination. This also mandates allowing and accepting our feelings without judging or condemning their rightness or wrongness — but just accepting that they are. They are the road map of our journey home. By judging their appropriateness and buying into our "should" system, we only detract our journey and sidestep our path to inner awareness.

An excellent exercise to affirm and expand our personal feelings of self-acceptance and love is created by Louise Hay in the book *You Can Heal Your Life* (Hay House, 1987). She believes that we can strengthen our love of self, and accept all of our feelings by talking to a mirror. With this process she believes that first we must be willing to change, and secondly, look ourself straight in the eye and lovingly accept through positive affirmations all the elements of ourself. By standing in front of a mirror and talking to ourself, we reflect the affirmation of acceptance of all of our feelings. She notes that the mirroring technique is a powerful tool because we have had most of our early negative messages given as others looked us straight in the eye. This process counterbalances our destructive messages and gives us the power over ourself to accept and love.

There is a big difference, however, between admittance and acceptance of our feelings. In the step of *admittance* we deal with our feelings in our head (logical thinking) but when we truly *accept* ourself, we love ourself with our heart. The mirror technique takes us into the realm of our inner strength and into our self-love.

My first and primary relationship is with myself. I have the awareness of my own needs and desires and can fully trust my inner guiding voice.

I am whole. I am complete. I am perfect just as I am right now.

Finding The Balance

Adult Children are familiar with the concept of black-or-white thinking. This phrase refers to a style of decision-making which sees only two available options in complete opposition in any situation. Examples of such choicemaking include either this or that, him or her, right or wrong and good or bad. This may include extremes such as "I must stay with him with no boundaries" or "I must leave him"; "I am completely right" or "I am completely wrong"; "I am all good", or "I am totally bad". Through awareness we learn that choices do not need to be at extremes. The concept of personal growth and enhancement explores the concept of looking at the greys or available options.

A similar concept of balance is described by a creative artist named Keith who explained, "It's not the greys that are in the middle — it's color — the color span between black and white which is technicolor." (White is the absence of color and black is the combination of all colors.) Keith's insight of absolutes can directly relate to relationships and finding our personal balance.

Just by reading this far, you have come to realize the technicolor beauty you hold within. As we continue along our journey, you will discover the magnificence that you hold locked inside you. As Louise Hay says, "You are not a helpless victim of your own thoughts, but rather a master of your own mind." *What you need, you will find!*

Our balance is found in the spectrum between not loving at all and loving too much. The technicolor foundation of loving is only possible when we take the focus off the extreme ends — that is, the focus off others. Technicolor implies a delicate balance between loving ourself and sharing our love with another. The real difficulty for most of us is finding that very delicate balance. Sometimes we find that we are symbolically a few hues too light or too dark. The balance comes by testing, carefully mixing, listening to our inner voice and feelings, using past information and believing in our personal talents and intuition.

Finding our own perfect hue mandates taking risks and being totally in touch with our inner guiding system. That inner guiding system allows us to trust our intuition, and our logical side provides us with the needed procedures to initiate action. Intuitively, we already know the way if we choose to actually feel our own inner guidance system.

Too many times we have abandoned our inner guidance (other examples of this guidance include names such as . . . our Inner Child, our Light, the God Within, our inner voice, etc.) and focus externally for our pathway to recovery. Our journey will be much easier if we trust the power we hold within our own self. But as we know, trusting ourself is extremely difficult for Children of Trauma. We have been taught that we cannot trust our intuition or gut feelings (despite their amazing reliability) and instead must make decisions in accordance with what is going on with others around us. We have been taught through years and years of practice to REACT in response to others' needs and REACT accordingly to please them. We learn to REACT from our heads (logic) in the hope of being capable enough to do it right. To our amazement, even though we have repeatedly seen its consequences, we find we never can do it just right.

We keep trying and trying to get what we need outside ourself. It is almost like going up to a brick wall and knocking our head against it. Time and time again our head bursts with pain. Our head bleeds profusely but we numb ourselves to our reality. We close our eyes and continue to bash our head over and over again in an attempt to be good enough. Disfigured and mentally defeated we lock ourselves into this destructive pattern without viewing the option of discontinuing our self-inflicted pain.

Sam, an over-responsible first child, attempted over and over again to gain the love and approval of his alcoholic father. He tried any and all means to satisfy and attain the approval of the one man who told him that he was not good enough. Consequently, filled with anguish and defeat, Sam discovered that he had no limits to prove to his dad his abilities, his accomplishments, his caring. Despite all the attempts, Sam still did not meet up to his father's unrealistic expectations (not that Sam ever knew just what those expectations really were). Rejected and dejected, Sam pushed himself into workaholism, perfectionism by completely shutting out the world around him in an attempt to prove the unprovable. By trying to please another person and meet someone else's expectations, Sam was helpless to ever prove he was good enough. His focus was externally derived, and he lost himself to live up to what he thought his dad wanted. By using this destructive process, he ignored the power he held within — the power of his inner guide who said he *was* good enough.

With any new technique, trusting our intuition takes awareness, allowing ourself to be vulnerable to taking risks and using the

Check System developed by Gravitz and Bowden. In their book, *Guide To Recovery,* they have popularized the "check system". The technique involves taking small risks and then standing back and FEELING (from your inner self) the results. By taking a risk and then checking the consequences and the results inside, we begin to become cautiously vulnerable, and take care of ourself at the same time.

The system involves a focus on ourself as we learn to read and understand ourself to the fullest. We become the navigator of our journey, learning to take small steps without violating our own personal boundaries. As we begin to claim our own identity, we are able to focus on our own growth and reclaim our boundaries. We make decisions in our life that take into account our needs, and do not allow ourself to put others first in our decision-making. This is not to say that we do not care for other people or that we do not take their feelings into account or listen to their wants. What we are saying is that for the first time, we check *our* feelings for our inner guidance and then make a decision that is healthy for *us.*

On her path to inner love Debbie described her technicolor balance as a place where you can see the positives of past relationships, and utilize them for your own personal growth. Debbie explored her vision of using relationships as a means of discovering clues about herself. She found it useful to recall relationships and discover what she had learned during the process. Each relationship uncovered a gift about herself and taught her a personal lesson about her individuality.

For instance, Debbie discovered in her relationship with her first lover that she was sensitive, caring and loving, an enhancement that made her special. She discovered in her relationship with her best friend that she could successfully tell someone about her needs, wants and feelings, and she could be heard. She learned that she could trust appropriate people in a safe healthy fashion. She learned in the relationship with her mother that she was quick-witted and had a delightful sense of humor that was appreciated and loved. By utilizing her experience, she became aware of her own uniqueness. Relationships became a *mirror* of her personal internal masterpiece — the amazing creation of her inner love.

By examining the past relationships in a positive manner, Debbie discovered the wonderful gifts she had within to share with others. Each gift is a hue of her technicolor rainbow that she can draw upon. By utilizing each hue in different and similar combinations she has been able to develop many beautiful and valuable relationships. The balance and proportion of each relationship may vary — no two relationships have the same elements, therefore, different needs and wants can be satisfied by different relationships.

A word of caution: The concept that Debbie described is only possible if the gifts which we hold within are illustrated on our canvas. If we try to paint a relationship by others' techniques, we lose our own gift of creativity and expression. Ironically, we lose what makes us unique and become a copy of the other person's expressions. People are drawn to our uniqueness, not our ability to copy someone else's masterpiece.

---■---

I am balanced and centered as I focus on myself.

I am whole. I am complete. I am perfect just as I am right now.

---■---

Mirroring

In a childhood story by Dina Anastasio called *The Magic Mirror* (Mirrors and Images, New York, 1986), a mother discovers in a small shop a beautiful antique mirror, which she proudly brings home to her family. The mirror becomes part of the family experience of viewing how they look to the outside world. The mirror reflected the feelings of each family member and gave everybody an insight into their being.

As the story progressed, the family began to use the mirror as a means to find the positive strengths within themselves. Everyone found the power they held within by confronting their fears in front of the powerful reflective mirror. They found themselves secretly talking to the mirror and creating the affirmations of what they wanted to find within. Without anyone else's knowledge, the mirror was a visual key to each one's personal growth. Consequently, the mirror became a friend and ally to practice newly learned behaviors, identify individualized positive attributes, practice affirmations and be the recipient of dreams which each one created. The mirror became almost mystical in nature because every family member found within it the magic of their own being. By the story's end, they realized that they had each created their own destiny and found the strength they had never known existed within themselves.

The contemporary usage of mirroring is beautifully described in Shakti Gawain's *Living in the Light* (Whatever Publisher, 1986), which involves a process in direct opposition to most Children of Trauma's relationship skills. For most of us, our concept of self-esteem and worth is attained and maintained by external forces outside ourself. We learned as children to be reactors and to calibrate our daily lives by the moods, trends and behaviors of our dysfunctional families. We were seldom, if ever, rewarded for individuality and personal growth as we attempted to reach self-actualization.

Typically a perfect example of this was the family scapegoat whose every attempt to gain an individual identity was met with negative feedback and who was characterized as the problem child. We became totally immersed and reinforced in our loss of self and learned to react to what was necessary to *survive* in our family. We reacted like the ball hooked by elastic to a paddle — the paddle moved and we reacted accordingly. It seems we bounced back and forth uncontrollably with no command of our movements. We found that reacting was our only means of survival. We found that we didn't *live* life . . . we only *survived* it.

Consequently we were taught that our relationships involve focusing outside ourself for confirmation of our love. If someone loves us, we are worthwhile. Without a relationship, we are nothing. Because of this distorted destructive logic, we are always out of control of our own being. We constantly find ourselves at the mercy of others. Consequently as we focus on others, we find that we ignore our own issues and relapse in our own personal recovery. By focusing on someone else, we lose sight of the real beloved: ourself. We tend to value the other person's affirmation and love as more valuable than the love of ourself. As the destructive cycle continues, we lose contact with our inner strength and our self-worth becomes **other-worth**. (Figure 3). We become a victim of our own creation. Perhaps this is best explained by a passage from Shirley MacLaine's *Dancing in the Light* (Bantam Books, 1983) ". . . We are not victims of the world we see . . . we are victims of the way we see the world." If we see the world through another, we are held captive in a prison of our own design.

Figure 3. Other Worth: The Vicious Cycle of Destruction

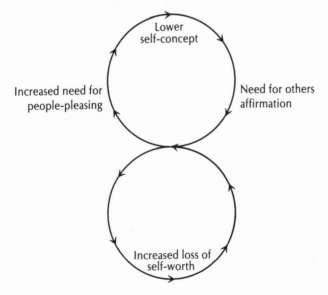

Lower
self-concept

Increased need for
people-pleasing

Need for others
affirmation

Increased loss of
self-worth

The Gift Of Self-Awareness

A loving friend named Pam shared her concept of healthy relationships in her life.

"For the first time I finally feel really comfortable with myself. I feel such inner calmness and serenity. I must be reflecting that to others because I feel so different. Consequently, I find that I am drawing healthy people toward me. It is remarkable that my attraction is not out of my neediness — but created by my recovery. I think I have learned the necessary lessons from my pain.

"In the past I needed a relationship where my self-worth was dependent on someone else precisely so I could see that I was living an illusion. Experiencing my co-dependent behavior in a primary relationship was the necessary path. Today I no longer have to stay in this classroom but can move along in my journey toward unconditional self-love. I am making choices that are good for me by facing my fear. I am now making changes in tune with my inner feelings and listening to my heart first."

The focus for Pam is quite different than most philosophies — she looks within to reflect on what she sees outside. This process teaches us that when we use the mirror, we can no longer damn the gods. We need to reflect on what is the lesson with this relationship or that situation that we need to learn. It's the difference between being a victim and being an investigator. An investigator asks what do I need to learn as if he is on a treasure hunt and is hungry for every clue. Most important, the really tough or painful clues are often the ones we have the most to learn from.

Many of us define ourself by the opposite — we look outside ourself to find out how others see us before deciding who we are. This may seem like a subtle difference, but it is the clue to the process of mirroring. By using the concept of mirroring, you can learn to utilize self-awareness by exploring what you experience in all of your relationships. The old destructive message in your head was, "You are what others think you are, and you are *not* what others think you are not." This distorted message kept us locked in a pattern of self-imprisonment and an internal craving for external validation and approval.

For most of us, trusting and loving ourself comes after working through loss and grief. It is almost like peeling away layers of an onion. Each layer is peeled away, and we come closer to finding the love inside. The onion is pungent in the beginning and there are a lot of tears and crying in the process. But as we peel away the layers of external focusing, we are amazed to find a magical surprise — inside the onion is a gorgeous fragrant center that is as magnificent as any rose. Its beauty is only experienced by those who dare to peel away the layers of the onion.

The process involves looking within and trusting your intuition. It also involves acceptance of all of your layers. Many of us allow our journey to end because we don't like what we find along the way. The trick is to remember the only way to get away from what is repulsive or painful to recognize is to love it and ourselves.

Only through unconditional acceptance can we expand and continue to grow. If we turn away from rejected parts of ourselves, the journey stops and the detour begins. The joy of self-love is not an overnight event, but it is a gradual awakening over a lifetime.

---■---

*I reflect the wisdom I find within. I am
open to the power within me.*

*I am whole. I am complete. I am perfect
just as I am right now.*

---■---

Falling In Love With Yourself

The concept of falling in love with yourself is a vague idea for most of us. We would gladly attempt this monumental feat of recovery if we only knew the how-to's of the process. Too often we are told about these nebulous suppositions without the road map that we desperately need. An excellent example is the popular terminology of recovery. We talk of this illusive notion without any insight of the means by which we could reach the goal. Most of us are confused about knowing if we are in recovery even when we come close. Because of the unclear jargon, we become depressed by our inability to be sure that we are nearing or have attained health and recovery. We find that we have difficulty seeing our progress, consequently we have difficulty seeing our power within.

Finding the love within you *mandates* the negation of your destructive message that you are unable to care for yourself. It necessitates the belief in your own personal power. This may be accomplished in many ways: by addressing your personal issues in therapy, joining an Adult Children of Alcoholics or Children of Trauma group, becoming part of a 12-Step program and/or utilizing a personal spirituality program.

The focus on a relationship with self must be the primary focus for this process's success. Each new accomplishment in our recovery promotes our trust in our power within. As personal grief and loss is addressed, we open to new aspects of ourself.

Sometimes the process is quite slow and tedious — a lot like working through a giant jawbreaker that we used to eat as kids. The jawbreaker was so large and overwhelming. We licked and licked the coating . . . sometimes to the point that our tongue was rough and sore from our persistence. But we kept on with our struggle to get to the middle. We knew the payoff was coming closer, and our wonderful surprise in the middle was just licks away. Realistically for most of us, the surprise in the middle was the reward of personal accomplishment and self-worth and the dedication to gain the reward inside. We believed in our perseverance and that the inner surprise was worth all the hard work and struggle. We learned to trust ourself and our ability to find what we were seeking. As we work through our stumbling blocks, we discover our power to heal ourselves. We begin to find a radiating energy which motivates us to continue searching for our personal gifts.

Laura, a remarkable Adult Child, described the rewards

as . . . "Floating on a puffy white cloud on my own power. I can't believe any drug could make me feel SO high!" Laura has found her inner gift of self-love using her world as a mirror for her recovery. As we journey forward, our path, like Laura's, teaches us the special skill of self-awareness and self-acceptance.

One of the most potent explanations of the process of self-understanding, self-awareness and self-love is described in Shakti Gawain's *Living in the Light*.

The tools below are integral components which can be used as a road map on your journey into personal understanding:

1. *"Everything in my life is my reflection, my creation."* If something outside myself has an effect on me, then it has a lesson for me to learn. It has been created and has relevance to me because it teaches me something about myself.

For instance, we may find that someone close to us tends to cause anxiety and anger within us. Perhaps it is because she is constantly caretaking and trying to be responsible for everyone in her life. Using the experience and the components of our feelings (anxiety and anger) as a lesson in our life, can we relate this to our own personal feelings of caretaking and over-responsibility? Perhaps we are jealous of the rewards and strokes that our friend attains from her caretaking action? Do we desire the attention that is directed at others who are cared for? As you can see, we use the process to address our own introspection and recovery as a means of learning about ourself.

With this technique we can keep a constant focus on our feelings, our needs and our wants, as well as our personal learning and growth. We can also become aware of our destructive thinking and our shame messages that lock us into ourself for satisfaction. This new frame of focusing keeps us directed at our feelings, not our "head" (logic, people-pleasing, caretaking, etc.), which has always been filled with distorted messages and rationalizations.

2. *"Everything is a gift that brings me to awareness."* Whether our reflection affects us positively or negatively, we must use everything as "classroom" material (classroom refers to life's lessons as part of our personal education) to learn what we need.

Many times as Children of Trauma, we find that we are repulsed by our negative feelings instead of using them as a gift to understand our personal journey. Our distaste of our negative feelings tends to encourage our feeling of self-destruction and failure. We must constantly be aware that our feelings are neither good nor bad, they just are. Without accepting the *full* spectrum of emotions, there can be no inner growth or self-awareness. Emotions are the key to unlocking our magnificent treasure chest of knowledge and self-love within us.

The two keys above will affirm your personal journey. However, many of us have not listened to the messages that we have within our reach. Previously we have gone outside ourself for esteem, worth and love. For the first time we have a method which focuses on our own being. With these two guidelines, we discover the power to be our own teacher, our own master and our own navigator. We learn to trust our own self and our intuition as we grow stronger in our personal journey in recovery.

Sadly many Children of Trauma find their strength within and then proceed to punish themselves for not finding the power sooner. We are so regimented that we *should have* done it faster, quicker or better. This *should of* thinking minimizes our process and decreases our ability to truly love ourself.

Because of our dysfunctional home of origin, we have been taught that everything that occurs in the world around us is our responsibility, rather than recognizing that it is only what we do with our experiences that are our responsibility. So we decide that surely our inability to discover and listen to our inner voice sooner proves our incompetence and lack of intelligence. We consistently see ourselves as failures because of our lack of being whole and perfect.

A passage from *Emmanuel's Book* addresses this issue with amazing sensitivity and understanding.

> *"With awareness you give yourself the gift*
> *of an opening for growth and change.*
> *Do not criticize yourself*
> *because in darkness you could not see.*
> *When you find the Light within you,*
> *you will know that you have always*
> *been in the center of wisdom.*
> *As you probe deeper into who you really are,*
> *with your lightedness and your confusion,*
> *with your angers, longings and distortions,*
> *you will find the true living God.*
> *Then you will say:*
> *'I have known you all of my life*
> *and I have called you by many different names.*

I have called you mother and father and child.
I have called you lover.
I have called you sun and flowers.
I have called you my heart.
But I never, until this moment,
called you Myself!' "

———————————————————■———————————————————

Today I will reflect upon my new insights and progress as I learn to love myself to the fullest.

I am whole. I am complete. I am perfect just as I am right now.

———————————————————■———————————————————

3

How Do We Get There?

You have courageously discovered *where you were,* and you now have some insights to *where you are going* in your relationship with yourself and others within your life. The following chapter will give you some basic hands-on information to assist you on your journey into self-acceptance and self-love. This is part of the process in attaining the wisdom of *how to get there* in your recovery.

The accumulation of ideas in this section is only a beginning spot along your journey to loving yourself and claiming your boundaries. But you must be on the lookout — you may find yourself nearing inner peace. This may pose a serious threat to the way things have been up to now — this is the new beginning of the New Loving You!

Some signs to alert you to inner peace

1. A tendency to listen to your heart and respond out of your needs and wants first and foremost, rather than on the basis of past experiences
2. An unmistakable ability to live life in the now

3. Feeling responsible for your own life
4. A loss of interest in judging and taking care of others
5. A loss of interest in judging yourself and now caring for yourself
6. A loss of interest in interpreting the actions of others
7. A loss of worry and a minimization of fear
8. Frequent overwhelming episodes of appreciation
9. Feelings of connectedness with nature and others
10. Frequent attacks of smiles
11. An increased tendency to let things happen, rather than making them happen
12. An increased susceptibility to love extended by others, as well as the uncontrollable urge to extend it
13. Feelings of being whole
14. Feelings of being complete
15. The belief that you are perfect just as you are right now.

Author unknown

You Get What You Got If You Do What You Did

An excellent tool in our recovery is the utilization of affirmations in our life. One of the best sources for such work has been developed by Rokelle Lerner. Her book *Daily Affirmations for Adult Children of Alcoholics* (Health Communications, 1985) can be used as a source of meditation, a focus for a morning inspiration or a focus for the day. Many of these affirmations specifically deal with relationship issues with others, but most importantly they all focus on relationship with ourself. As we become more in tune with our own being, this type of sourcebook is a vital part of our recovery process.

The following example of an affirmation from Rokelle Lerner's book is an excellent starting place for our next worksheet. On May 2 she writes the following affirmation concerning relationships:

Whenever I enter into a relationship with the idea that another person can make me happy and content, I have begun to fail in that relationship. When I view a relationship in this way, I become concerned over what I might or might not get back.

Today I release my pattern of someone's having to live up to my ideal. I have no right to impose my performance requirements on anyone else.

Today I start relieving others of the responsibility for making me happy. In this way I can begin intimate relationships based upon mutual caring, not on need. This day I acknowledge that I am a full, rich and complete person.

I deserve a relationship, not to make me happy, but to share the richness of who I am in totality with another.

As we move forward, we must allow ourself the time to reflect upon our past to see where we have been, so we may create where we are going in the now.

A common slogan utilized in recovery and used earlier in this book is *IF YOU DO WHAT YOU DID, YOU GET WHAT YOU GOT!* This philosophy is an excellent starting point to relate your personal patterns of relationships.

To identify our patterns, it is useful to look at the past to evaluate more specifically our personal issues. A useful means to seek this information is by discovering our patterns, attitudes and values. Many times such information is requested in books, but many times we do not allow ourself the luxury of working through such exercises but merely skim their content. Because you have come to this point of your recovery, you have come to realize the importance of fully exploring such issues in your life. You have discovered that you no longer want what you got — you have *done* what you *did* long enough. Now is time for the changes in your life. Take the time now to assist your journey and answer the following questions within the pages of this book, or use the questions for your daily journaling.

What was your specific pattern of relationships in the past?

What type of person did you attract?

How did your loving pattern fit in with the characteristics listed in the first chapter?

What are your expectations of your lover?

What are your expectations of your friends?

What are your expectations of your children?

What are your expectations of your parents?

What are your expectations of yourself with your lover?

What are your expectations of yourself with your friends?

What are your expectations of yourself with your children?

What are your expectations of yourself with your parents?

What patterns would you like to change in your life?

What changes can you create to become more loving and accepting of yourself?

These questions can help you on your journey. They are a starting point for exploration forward. They will allow you to focus on yourself, not on others. This information will then assist you with the remainder of your journey to find the strength within. As you explore the questions above, be gentle and loving with yourself. You must understand that you are at a new beginning in your life. Give yourself patience, kindness and love. You are the greatest love in your life.

———————————————■———————————————

*Today is a new beginning. I will make
positive changes in my life to create
a loving self.*

*I am whole. I am complete. I am perfect
just as I am right now.*

———————————————■———————————————

The 10 Demandments

As we explore our relationships, we have placed many expectations on ourself as well as on others in our life. We explored the concept of our expectations of ourself and others using the worksheet.

As we uncover our expectations of others, we realize how we have sabotaged our relationship with ourself. We have discovered that we have allowed others to rule our life and our destiny. Today we are changing. Each day is becoming easier because we are aware of where we have been and where we are going.

The following 10 Demandments were created by an anonymous author. They can be used to illustrate how we have created destructive addictive relationships in the past. Living by the premises written in these Demandments will surely insure being locked in our external focusing with our ultimate loss of self.

As you read the following, realize how far we have traveled in our journey together. We have broken some of our shackles that had bound us in our relationships.

The 10 Demandments

10 Rules To Live By To Insure Unhappiness In A Relationship

1. Thou shalt make me happy.
2. Thou shalt not have any interests other than me.
3. Thou shalt know what I want and what I feel without me having to say.
4. Thou shalt return each one of my sacrifices with an equal or greater sacrifice.
5. Thou shalt shield me from anxiety, worry, hurt or any pain.
6. Thou shalt give me my sense of self-worth and esteem.
7. Thou shalt be grateful for everything I do.
8. Thou shalt not be critical of me, show anger toward me or otherwise disapprove of anything I do.
9. Thou shalt be so caring and loving that I need never take risks or be vulnerable in any way.
10. Thou shalt love me with thy whole heart, thy whole soul and thy whole mind, even if I do not love myself.

———————————————— ■ ————————————————

*Today I give myself the gift of change. I
have discarded the destructive
bonds that have held me captive in
relationships.*

*I am whole. I am complete. I am perfect
just as I am right now.*

———————————————— ■ ————————————————

Relationship Boundaries

Reclaiming our personal boundaries has allowed us the freedom to focus on our relationship with ourself. In the past our focusing on others had caused us to enmesh with others, consequently we lost ourself. With the realization of our self-destruction, we have become aware of our need to care and love ourself and set limitations with our boundaries. This does not necessitate living our lives *totally* focused on our own self. It is not necessary to become egocentric to begin to love and care for ourself.

One common concern of many of us, who claim our own boundaries, is the feeling of guilt and selfishness. For us, this is the first time in our life that we have allowed ourself the luxury to care for our own self.

An Adult Child named Sue told her support group that she felt guilty and disgraceful because she was looking at her own needs and *not* those of other people.

"I feel narcissistic. All of my childhood I was told to stop thinking only of myself." She continued exploring the old message which set up these feelings of shame. She discovered that the message had been pounded deep into her head that she MUST care for others first and primarily. She was instructed that caring for herself was a form of being self-centered and inconsiderate of other people's feelings and needs. A good girl should (and must) put others first. This philosophy, of course, mandated that she put herself last. Her message from her home of origin was effectively sabotaging any progress in which she reclaimed her own needs, wants and desires. The conflicts between her old destructive message (from her home of origin) and her recovery was in complete opposition. This conflict of inner messages held Sue from truly loving and accepting herself at the deepest level.

Claiming our personal boundaries does not imply that other people are not vital to our lives, but it does mean that we must love ourself *before* we can fully love others. Such love does not mandate that we go to a distant mountain top, live on a deserted island, become a cave-dwelling hermit, contact a guru (the guru is in you) or break from all loved ones. On the contrary, personal growth means maintaining relationships with others or we will never have the opportunity to test our boundaries. We need others to learn fully our lessons and assist our mirroring processes. We can reclaim our boundaries and allow positive people in our life who can help support and assist us. These people nurture and assist our growth process, but do not ask us to give ourself away to attain their love. In other words, for the first time our love is not conditional. Now we come to the realization that we were the ones who made our love conditional internally.

The significant people in our life reap the benefits of our new found strength within. Others gain because as we love ourself, we radiate an energy of caring and balance. Our energy is freer and more flowing because we are not giving away all we have to others. We are living in the moment, in full contact with our needs, our wants and our desires.

Let's imagine a brilliant vibrant illuminating sun. Its radiation spreads its sunrays far into the galaxy. The light and warmth are felt by all that make contact with the blazing star. Symbolically, we *are* that shining sun — we have the energy and source to radiate our beauty, our warmth and produce magnificent proportions of personal enlightenment.

The sun's formation required clouds of gases and dust. Without these elements there was no possibility of the star's full potential. Our formation is quite similar in nature. We are an internal furnace of glowing light which comes from the love within. The blazing fire is created as a source of energy which can be directed toward our own creative love.

We radiate our splendor because we are in touch with our inner self. In the past when we focused on others, we were forced to shut down our strength and power internally, and give ourself away. We became dead and empty. We were like a star that had given all it could give and had burned out. We locked the door to our potential.

Just as the sun needed clouds of gas, dust and the forces of nature to produce its illuminating brilliance, we too are in need of other elements to brighten our life. The enhancement of others is what reflects the magnificence that we radiate. Some people enhance our lives as aquaintances, some as friends, some as lovers, some as intimate companions. Some relationships are conflicts and struggles and we are tempted to run from them. They too are enhancements IF we choose to accept the lessons they contain. We have many people who touch our lives in many different and unique forms. Each enhancer has the potential to reflect our gift of love that we have found within ourself.

Once again let's imagine the analogy of ourself as the radiating sun. We hold with us powerful blazing strength, vibrant warmth and inner love that make us an iridescent power within our universe. We are at peace with ourself and have successfully defined our boundaries. We no longer need to focus on others. We have come to define what we hold within and no longer need to fix, take care of or externally live our lives through others.

As the middle of our universe (Figure 4), we radiate outward to the relationships that surround us. The closest rings to our boundary are the most intimate people in our lives. As we move outward from the center circles, we include those people who are less intimate to experience our radiating forces of love and warmth. We have come to realize that everyone does not belong in our innermost circle, and we do not need to enmesh with all the people in our life.

Figure 4. Our Universe

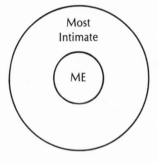

Within this closest circle to our boundaries, we include the people who we feel most comfortable with to share our most intimate personal feelings and ourself. We feel safety in that sharing and rejoice in the radiation that we give to them, as they reflect their love and support to us. Please note that there may be more than one person within this closest ring — perhaps your significant other, your spouse, your lover, your dearest intimate friend, your children, etc. It is imperative to realize that each person can share and utilize different radiations that you transmit. For instance, one person may share your intimate feelings concerning your spirituality. Another intimate person in your life may be allowed to share your feelings concerning your recovery, your transformation with your relationship issues, as well as your sexual expression. Both people can be within the same ring but experience different aspects of your inner sanctuary.

It is useful to realize that this illustration of our relationship boundaries is quite different from that of an addictive, destructive relationship. The rings of the addictive relationship are not as defined nor are the boundaries as clear. In fact, the rings are enmeshed in nature. It is hard to see where we begin and where we stop. For that matter, it is difficult to find where we stop and the other person begins. There is so much externalization that we have disconnected from within. We have become the enabler of others' lives and have lost our inner focus.

Figure 5. Unhealthy Relationships (Enmeshed)

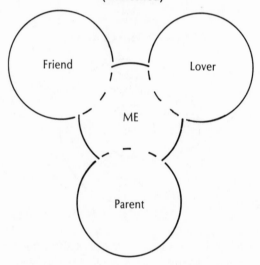

In our healthy relationships we move outward with our radiation, as we allow other people to share our warmth. As we move further out, we include people who are less intimate in our lives, and those with whom we have more defined boundaries. Each person enhances our life. Each person finds safety in knowing our boundaries, as we feel safety in the declaration of our independence and freedom from enmeshment and externalization. Each person reflects a different aspect of our life.

The next radiating boundary might include people with whom we would share some specific aspects of our personal life. As the circles radiate out, our availability to be vulnerable with those people decreases.

Figure 6. Healthy Relationships

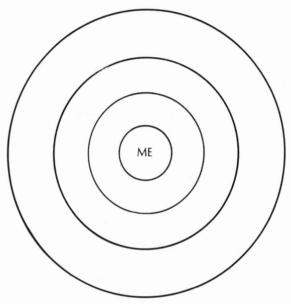

Within this process it is possible for people to radiate in and out of each boundary at different times. There is flexibility for movement inward and outward. At times we may choose to let someone become closer to ourself and later decide that they need to be placed further out in our boundary rings. The opposite may occur and we may decide to allow someone to move closer within our more intimate rings, as we develop more trust in that person.

As you can see, as we become stronger and more in touch with our love of self, we have more to radiate outward. Our boundaries create a means of guiding healthy relationships by evaluating who is allowed into specific parts of our life.

The following is a relationship boundary worksheet for use in your life. It will be useful to you to write in this book and identify the people who occupy the intimacy rings of your life. For the sake of sorting, it might be useful to also note by the side of each person, what specific issues you feel comfortable sharing with that person. This sorting process helps us realize how each person enhances our life, and the specific vulnerability we have

established with each person. This sorting also helps us redefine
and reclaim our boundaries by exploring our relationships.

Figure 7. Personal Diagram of Relationship Boundaries

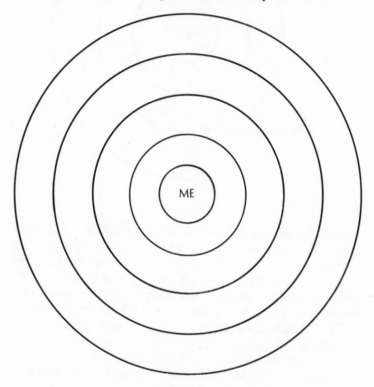

We can create healthy relationships in our life. We have reclaimed ourself and our personal boundaries.

I am whole. I am complete. I am perfect, just as I am right now.

Daily Progress Worksheet

As the baggage falls by the wayside, we feel the freedom of today and the hope for tomorrow. By making changes, we create a lifetime change. Each step takes us closer to believing that we are enough and deserve our own love and acceptance.

A key to self-awareness is a means of maintaining and promoting a daily inventory of our progress along our journey. How many times along our path have we been unaware of how we created our pain or pleasure? A daily inventory worksheet gives us a useful process to assess our feelings, values, behavioral progress, success and failures (the term failure is meant to imply roadblocks versus a negative condemnation of one's self).

By targeting our goals we create an affirmation of our success in our todays and tomorrows. We create our destiny by allowing our dreams, aspirations and hopes to become part of our reality. An essential portion of our journey is the *belief* that we can attain what we desire. Our vision becomes our reality as we journey forward in personal recovery. You have come to realize that you have all the tools that you desire within your own heart. We now are assured that our first step was the belief in our own strength and the love of our own self.

Usage Of The Worksheet

The following worksheet (page 85) is a simple, quick method of recording our daily progress. The **Issue To Be Addressed** can be any relevant issue in your life. Some have found it useful to utilize a portion of Rokelle Lerner's *Daily Affirmations* (Health Communications, 1985) book as a daily focus. Other sources of affirmations or goals may come from *The Journey Within* (Health Communications, 1987), *Time For Joy* (Health Communications, 1988), *Living in the Light* (Whatever Publisher, 1986), *Emmanuel's Book* or a step from our first book *Following the Yellow Brick Road* (Health Communications, 1988). Perhaps it would be even more useful to devise one of your own creation with a special meaning for you. The source is not as important as the commitment to the creation for personal change. The **GOAL** is a statement of a behavioral change that you wish to make.

Many times we repeat old behaviors as a means of dealing with current decision-making processes. Earnie Larsen, in *Stage II Recovery*, (Winston Press, 1985), states that 95% of what we do is created out of habit. No wonder we have a difficult time breaking destructive patterns. By utilizing the resources of evaluating our past behaviors and feelings, we have a guidepost of our habits (and our feelings) and what we have created as a positive change. With this information, we have insight into what has **worked** and **failed,** as well as our feelings concerning those events. This is another check-and-balance system in our recovery process. The **plan of action** gives us a specific path for our journey. The **progress** of our **behaviors** and feelings allows us to take a daily inventory of our progress. Typically, we have been trained to see only weaknesses and failures. This process focuses on our successes and our strengths within to be utilized in our journey. The development of our self-enhancement is added by the affirmation of our process. **Tomorrow's plan of attack** allows us the foresight to see our recovery as a journey *not* a destination.

The following is an example of a completed Daily Progress Worksheet. We have included a blank sheet for you to copy for your own daily use or as a format for part of your daily journaling.

As you become in touch with yourself, you become more accepting and loving of your own radiating being. You are making a change that makes a lifetime difference!

Example Of Daily Progress Worksheet

Issue To Be Addressed: Caretaking.

Goal: Focus on *my* needs, wants, desires and not others.

Things That I Have Tried Before That Have Worked: I have been conscious of my behavior with over-responsibility with jobs at work and at home; I have intervened with my behavior by using positive statements of affirmation; I have used meditation for focusing on my goal.

My Feelings Concerning That Action: Positive self-worth; powerful; hopeful.

Things That I Have Tried Before That Have Failed: Talking to my husband about his irresponsibility; doing it all; complaining.

My Feelings Concerning That Failure: Low self-worth, trapped, degraded.

Plan Of Action For Attaining My Goal (Note things to watch out for): I will take time in the morning to focus on my goal during meditation; I will use my journaling time to write of the progress that I have made during the day; I will attempt to intervene with my behavior of caretaking; I will work on setting boundaries in my job and at home. I will be watchful of my need to gain strokes for doing it all.

Summarize Specific Behavioral Characteristics Concerning Today's Progress: I became aware of how I enable my co-worker to be irresponsible with her paperwork and then cover up for her mistakes; I became aware of how I am over-responsible and enabling to my child with chores at home.

Feelings Concerning The Progress Made Toward My Goal: I feel centered, balanced and more aware of my potential.

Plan Of Attack For Tomorrow: Look at my people-pleasing issues and my inability to say no.

Daily Progress Worksheet

_____ Date

Issue To Be Addressed _____

Goal _____

Things That I Have Tried Before That Have Worked _____

_____

_____

_____

My Feelings Concerning That Action _____

_____

_____

Things That I Have Tried Before That Have Failed _____

_____

_____

My Feelings Concerning That Failure _____

_____

_____

Plan Of Action For Attaining My Goal (Note things to watch out

for) _____

_____

_____

Summarize Specific Behavioral Characteristics Concerning Today's

Progress _____

_____

Feelings Concerning The Progress Made Toward My Goal _____

_____

_____

_____

Plan Of Attack For Tomorrow _____

_____

_____

Today I will see where I have been, where I am now and where I am going.

I am whole. I am complete. I am perfect just as I am right now.

Feelings Worksheet

Along our journey we have repeatedly encountered the core issue of our stuffed frozen feelings. As Adult Children of Alcoholics or Children of Trauma, we have entrapped our emotions tightly within us. Fear and trauma created the illusion within that our feelings were our "arch enemies" and they must be controlled. From our earliest memories we have had negative experiences that have created our need to control and suppress our feelings. Many of us were told not to talk to anyone about our secrets, and not to trust anyone outside our family (we discovered it also meant within our family). Some of us saw emotional release that was expressed through rage and violence, which taught us that we could not control or trust our feelings. Because of denial which masked what was occurring within our homes (hiding the secrets), many of us were taught that what we saw and felt was not accurate or acceptable.

As part of our recovery we have addressed our distorted home of origin thinking and have begun to open our hearts to our full potential. As we have allowed our emotions to evolve into a meaningful expression of ourself, we have blossomed. We have discovered that emotions are not something we must fear — they need to be embraced.

In the past our addictive relationship was our only means of feeling love in our life. Now we can look inside and gather what we need from within. As we accept and cherish our full range of emotions, we become more intuned with the full spectrum of what we can experience.

The following cartoon faces are a creative method to explore some of our emotions. The cartoons allow us a nonthreatening means of viewing how we look in each emotional state. The characters are a useful means of back-tracking which emotions we have experienced (and when) and which we have not experienced at all. These can be used as a treatment plan, per se, to work on the development of specific feelings we would like to incorporate in our life. We can then develop a plan of action to attain this feeling.

For example, Cindy, an Adult Child, had not experienced the feeling of joy. Her therapy group supported her goal of finding the joy within her. They worked with her to develop a plan of action to experience the joy within. Joy was felt and embraced when Cindy planned to spend time with her niece and nephew who she dearly loved. She allowed herself to feel fully the love that they shared. They gave her their love freely as she permitted herself to be a child and play with them in the park on a sunny spring afternoon. Totally vulnerable and not threatened by taking risks, Cindy felt what she had inside her that had been waiting for the blossoming occasion.

As we become more in touch with our feelings, we open ourself up to the potential for greater personal love. We find self-acceptance and discover that our energy flows when we break through to loving ourself completely.

Figure 8. How Do You Feel Today?

BASHFUL   DISAPPROVING

HURT   DISAPPOINTED   ANXIOUS   DISGUSTED   CONCENTRATING   HAPPY

CAUTIOUS   EXHAUSTED   FRUSTRATED   GUILTY   HUNGOVER   AGONIZED   AGGRESSIVE

Figure 8. How Do You Feel Today?   (Continued)

DEMURE   ENVIOUS

CONFIDENT   CURIOUS   COLD   ARROGANT   TIRED   ENRAGED

BLISSFUL   DETERMINED   GRIEVING   HORRIFIED   DISBELIEVING   APOLOGETIC   ECSTATIC

Gay Hendricks, in *Learning To Love Yourself, A Guide To Becoming Centered* (Prentice Hall Press, 1982), creates an excellent guide for understanding the transition from the non-experience to self-acceptance.

Non-experience:

1. Hoping you can love yourself
2. Wishing you could love yourself
3. Deciding you will love yourself
4. Believing that you should love yourself
5. Reasoning that you are loveable.

Self-acceptance:

6. Accepting things the way they are (afraid of loving yourself, looking at what holds you back, etc.)
7. Being willing to personally experience loving yourself
8. Being willing to be the source of love for yourself and others.

As we have discovered within these pages, your progress hinges on your experiencing that you are the source of your love. You internally create love and you do not need to go outside yourself to fill your emptiness. Your emotions, therefore, were always safe within you, because you held the key to inner love and the master key to accepting all of your emotions totally and completely.

I am at peace with my emotions. I accept and embrace all emotions and use them to discover my true love within.

I am whole. I am complete. I am perfect just as I am right now.

Breaking Distorted Shame Messages
(A Different Type Of 12 Steps)

Many times along our journey home we are halted by the accouterment of our excess baggage — our distorted shame messages. We carry this baggage like a ball and chain around our very being, beginning from our home of origin. The burden of negativity becomes heavier and heavier. As we trudge along our path, we become aware of the destructive potential of these messages. We discover that all our baggage is hanging around us like a traveler overwhelmed with tote bags, suitcases and satchels — each with the potential to hold back our passage forward.

The process of loving ourself involves first being aware of our destructive messages. Secondly, it mandates a procedure to break the hold of the captor — our perpetuation of these distorted shame messages. As we uncover these two aspects, we will feel disloyal, selfish or perhaps undeserving of discarding this baggage. Consequently, most of us are scared of what we might find inside each of our heavy suitcases. Our fear and doubt of that hidden baggage has locked us in our self-destruction, dependency and self-hatred our entire life. We have become so used to the pain and weight of our baggage that we feel uncomfortable with the thought of letting it go. But the letting go is an emancipation process toward real personal freedom and a means to loving ourself. This is one way to become all we were really meant to be.

Take your time and allow yourself patience as you utilize this step. Our shame messages have become embedded deep within. Breaking the destruction of their hold will involve constant vigilance and practice. Please do not expect perfection the first time through the following exercise. This is a process not an end point.

Remember you have given yourself permission to go this far. You have all you need within. The hold that comes from your destructive messages lies in the past. You are responsible and in control of today and this moment.

The following worksheet is a constructive means of working through distorted shame messages. It is necessary to utilize our feelings and inner guiding system to help us free ourself.

A Guided Example Of Usage Of The Distorted
Shame Message Worksheet

Many Children of Trauma have the distorted shame message that they are not good enough. This may manifest in a variety of forms: "I am responsible for my family's alcoholism because I was a failure"; "I did not produce enough"; "I am not worthy enough to have happiness"; "I should have done more"; "I am attracted to dysfunctional partners because I deserve nothing better." These messages will be our starting point to explore our 12-Stage worksheet. A blank worksheet is provided for your own useage on page 99.

It will be useful to make your shame distorted message (Stage I) as precise or specific as possible. By limiting our message we focus more directly on the distortion. Instead of "I'm not good enough", let's change the message to . . . "I'm not good enough as an adult in my roles (wife, mother, daughter, employee, etc.) . . ."

Stage 1: I'm not good enough today in my role.

Stage 2: Focuses on the origins of these messages —

      1. childhood — father

      2. childhood — mother

      3. childhood — grandmother

      4. childhood — Second grade teacher

Stage 3: Shame experiences — (This example is a shortened version. It will be helpful to write more on each topic to fully explore emotions.) As we write our experiences, we allow the feelings to escape and take away their power. We process our pain, despair, anger and hurt as we return to the emotional starting point. As we get in touch with these emotions, we break through our denial and lessen our trauma's hold on our today. Writing is an effective process for this necessary step.

      1. Remembrances of my father saying I was going to be the "death of him" because of my acting-out behavior. *I felt responsible and guilty.*

      2. Remembrances of my father saying that I never could do anything right. *I felt bad and shameful.*

      3. Remembrances of my mother saying I was "moody" and always "a pain" to take anywhere. *I felt hurt and useless.*

      4. Remembrances of my mother saying nothing was ever "good enough to suit me." *I felt misunderstood and dirty.*

5. Remembrances of my grandmother saying I should be more like my brother because he always does what he is told. *I felt that I was an embarrassment to the family.*

6. My teacher in the second grade telling me that I will not amount to anything because I'm always goofing off! I felt like a failure. *I felt worthless and not worthy of living.*

Stage 4: Feelings experienced —

1. Shame	7. Undeserving
2. Embarrassment	8. Dirty
3. Anger	9. Misunderstood
4. Hurt	10. Trapped
5. Suicidal	11. Worthless
6. Useless	12. Frightened

Stage 5: Most current stimuli to trigger old distorted messages —

1. Husband told me that it is my fault that the children are undisciplined. If I were better as a wife, our children would act better, be smarter and more creative.

2. Husband stated that my family is so messed up, no wonder I can't do anything right.

3. If I were better as a wife, my husband would not have to drink.

Stage 6: Current feelings —

1. Despair	4. Trapped
2. Helplessness	5. Anger
3. Hopelessness	6. Shame

Stage 7: How this message is destructive to me —

1. This creates emotional turmoil — feelings of depression, helplessness, hopelessness, despair, etc.

2. I notice that I am experiencing stomach pains (development of ulcer).

3. Once again feeling lower back pain (constant and extreme at times).

4. I am overweight (nurturing myself with food to numb the pain of the situation around me).

5. I am becoming a workaholic. (I realize that I am compulsive about finishing my work to get external praise.)

6. I am constantly a people-pleaser. (I can't say no to people even when it hurts me. I am afraid no one will approve of or like me unless I please them.)

Stage 8: New message creation —

I am capable of and willing to make changes in my life. I deserve to be free of my distorted messages and this baggage from my home of origin. I am capable of making those changes in my life today. I am worthwhile. I am whole. I am complete. I am perfect just as I am right now. I have no limitations, only myself.

Stage 9: New affirmations —

1. I *am* enough, just as I am.

2. I *am* deserving of what I create for myself.

3. It is okay for me to care and love myself.

Stage 10: Plan of attack —

Behavioral

1. I will make others responsible for their own actions. I will become aware and attempt to discontinue my enabling of others' irresponsibility (friends, workers, family).

2. I will begin standing up for myself by being assertive and walking away from verbal abuse.

3. I will decrease my overtime at work this week and work regularly scheduled hours.

4. I will exercise two times this week for 15 to 20 minutes.

5. I will state affirmations two times per day while looking in the mirror.

6. I will meditate each day in the morning before breakfast.

7. I will journal each night before I go to sleep.

8. I will utilize the Daily Progress Sheet as part of my journaling.

Attitude

1. I have come to the realization that I can only love and please myself.

2. I have come to realize that I must please myself before I can please anyone else.

3. I have come to realize that I am worth time, energy and my own love.

Verification/Validity Of My Accomplishments

1. I have become aware of my inner peace and serenity. I am sensing a change within.

2. I have had a decrease in my weight.

3. I have noticed a decrease in physical pains in my back and stomach.

4. I have feelings of freedom. I do not feel helpless and hopeless.

Stage 11: Added enhancement/Letting go —

1. I have a desire to further explore my boundaries and limits with significant relations (work, family, spouse).

2. I am mourning my losses and celebrating the transformation from the old me into the new me.

3. I will let go of shoulds and baggage from my family of origin which have kept me entrapped.

Stage 12: Celebration —

1. I will write a thank you to myself in my journal.

2. I will write down my progress for the day and week and celebrate my successes.

3. I will share my progress with my group members.

4. I will take time to use meditation as a means of seeing the Light within to foster my healing.

BREAKING DISTORTED SHAME MESSAGES WORKSHEET

STAGE 1 shame message/ distorted	STAGE 2 the origins/ reinforcements	STAGE 3 shame experiences/past remembrances
1.	1.	1.
2.	2.	2.
3.	3.	3.

STAGE 4 feelings during past events	STAGE 5 current stimulus to distorted messages	STAGE 6 current feelings to this message
1.	1.	1.
2.	2.	2.
3.	3.	3.

STAGE 7 how destructive/ how it hurts me	STAGE 8 new message created for self	STAGE 9 new affirmations
1.	1.	1.
2.	2.	2.
3.	3.	3.

STAGE 10 behavioral	STAGE 10 attitude	STAGE 10 verification
1.	1.	1.
2.	2.	2.
3.	3.	3.

STAGE 11 enhancements/let go		STAGE 12 celebration of process
1.		1.
2.		2.
3.		3.

As I break the messages that bind me, I become more loving and realize the possibilities of my full potential.

I am whole. I am complete. I am perfect just as I am right now.

Chapter One — Your Story

Robert Frost's poem, *The Road Not Taken,* symbolically illustrates our journey down the road to recovery. We choose the path that many dare not travel . . . the path to inner love and personal awareness. Our journey has led us home to our own inner child and taught us to recognize our own limits and reclaim our boundaries. We have dared to take the path "less traveled by, and it has made all the difference".

Visualize yourself standing at the crossroad of your journey. The path to the left takes you down the comfortable old way you have always known. The right path does not have a clearing (there are unknowns ahead). You know that the journey will be more challenging if you move to the right, and somehow you know you will find what you need down this pathway. Instinctively you follow your heart and march forward. Your fears and doubts fade into submission as you follow your own creation of your future. Boldly you pursue your journey past the limits that had always held you captive. Onward you travel facing each crossroad along the way as you become more and more aware of your strength, and you become more sure of the love you hold inside for yourself. As you move forward, you come to realize that you have *never* been alone. You were just in the "darkness". You always had yourself . . . all you needed to do was to trust and go forth.

As this vision fades from your memory, it now becomes time to write your own story. This is the time for your *own* Chapter One. It is the beginning of the "new you". Begin your novel . . . the epic story which is created, performed and directed by the greatest love of all . . . **you!** With the love we have found within, we realize that we are capable of unconditional love for ourself just as we are right now. For we are truly whole. We are complete. And we are perfect just as we are right now. We have realized that we have claimed the greatest gift we had to offer to anyone — ourself.

The sun rises over our home with the magnificence of the morning light. Its colors exemplify the aura of our strength. Inner peace and serenity fill our body that once held such emptiness. We are no longer lonely because we have found what we have searched so long to find — our self. At home with our own being, we are now confident to write our own saga. We are within the flow of life, and have found our limitless boundaries of self-love because we have claimed our boundaries. Only our *thoughts limit* our possibilities. The dreams we hold within our heart become the vision of our tomorrows. Alan Cohen's *Rising in Love* (Alan Cohen Publications, 1983) teaches us a valuable lesson: "We have to be willing to celebrate our own self coming around the bend before we can actually see it. We have to take a chance on ourselves making it."

With your pen in hand take some time to write an affirmation of the creation of your future. We bring to ourself what we dream . . . what we love . . . and what we need. Affirm your journey and the life you are creating on the following page.

My Novel

AFFIRM: *I will allow myself to effortlessly and peacefully write my story as a creation for my today. I write and affirm this so I may have the life I desire for my tomorrows.*

You have come to discover your inner strength and claimed your personal boundaries. You have all you need to create the life you desire. Share with me an affirmation for our today and tomorrows . . .

■

I only attract loving people in my world, for they are a mirror of what I am. I love myself, therefore, I forgive and totally release the past and all past experiences, and I am free. I love myself, therefore, I live totally in the now,. experiencing each moment as good and knowing my future is bright and joyous and secure . . .

Louise Hay, *You Can Heal Your Life*

■

Suggested Reading

Black, C. **It Will Never Happen to Me**, 1981. **Repeat After Me**, Denver: Medical Administration, 1985.

Carnes, P. **The Sexual Addiction**, Minneapolis: CompCare, 1983.

Cohen, Alan. **Rising in Love: The Journey into Light**, Cohen Publications, 1983.

Cowan, C.; Kinder, M. **Smart Women, Foolish Choices**, New York: Signet Classics, 1985.

Deutsch, C. **Broken Bottles, Broken Dreams**, New York: Teachers College Press, 1982.

Emmanuel's Book (Channeled by Pat Rodegast). New York: Bantam Books, 1985.

Fishel, Ruth. **The Journey Within: A Spiritual Path To Recovery**, 1987. **Learning to Live in the Now: 6 Week Personal Plan to Recovery**, 1988. **Time For Joy: Daily Affirmations**, Deerfield Beach: Health Communications, 1988.

Fisher, B. **Rebuilding**, San Luis Obispo: Impact Publications, 1981.

Fossom, M.; Mason, M. **Facing Shame: Families in Recovery**, New York: W.W. Norton, 1986.

Gawain, S. **Living in the Light**, San Rafael: Whatever Publications, 1986.

Gravitz, H.L.; Bowden, J.D. **Guide to Recovery: A Book for Adult Children of Alcoholics**, Holmes Beach: Learning Publications, 1985.

Halpern, H. **How to Break Your Addiction to a Person**, New York: Bantam Books, 1982.

Hay, L. **You Can Heal Your Life**, Santa Monica: Hay House, 1984.

Hendricks, G. **Learning to Love Your Self: A Guide To Becoming Centered**, New York: Prentice Hall, 1982.

Kiley, D. **The Wendy Dilemma**, New York: Avon Books, 1984.

Kritsberg, W. **Adult Children of Alcoholics Syndrome: From Discovery to Recovery**, Pompano Beach: Health Communications, 1986.

Larsen, E. **Stage II Recovery**, Minneapolis: Winston Press, 1985.

Lerner, R. **Daily Affirmations For Adult Children of Alcoholics**, Pompano Beach: Health Communications, 1985.

MacLaine, S. **Out On A Limb**, Toronto: Bantam Books, 1983.

Miller, J.; Ripper, M. **Following The Yellow Brick Road: The Adult Child's Personal Journey Through Oz**, Pompano Beach: Health Communications, 1988.

Norwood, R. **Women Who Love Too Much**, New York: Pocket Books, 1985.

O'Gorman, P.; Oliver-Diaz, P. **Breaking the Cycle of Addiction: For Adult Children of Alcoholics**, Pompano Beach: Health Communications, 1987.

Russionoff, P. **Why Do I Think I am Nothing Without a Man?** New York: Bantam Books, 1981.

Schaef, A.W. **Co-Dependence: Misdiagnosed and Mistreated**, Minneapolis: Winston Press, 1986.

Subby, R. **Lost in the Shuffle: The Co-dependent Reality**, Pompano Beach: Health Communications, 1987.

Wegscheider, S. **Another Chance: Hope and Health for the Alcoholic Family**, Palo Alto: Science and Behavior Books, 1981. **The Miracle**, Deerfield Beach: Health Communications, 1989.

Whitfield, C. **Healing the Child Within**, Pompano Beach: Health Communications, 1987.

Woititz, J. **Adult Children of Alcoholics**, 1983. **Struggle for Intimacy**, Pompano Beach: Health Communications, 1985.